International Law and Human Rights

International Law and Human Rights

by

Meenakshi Arora

SUMIT ENTERPRISES

New Delhi – 110 002

First Published 2010

ISBN : 978-81-8420-409-4

Published by :

SUMIT ENTERPRISES

4649B/21, Ansari Road, Darya Ganj
New Delhi-110002
Phones: 23279353, 9810217567
E-mail: Sumit_enterprises2007@yahoo.com

PRINTED IN INDIA

Published by Sri Lokesh Gupta for Sumit Enterprises,New Delhi-110002, Typeset by Graphic Era, Printed at Nav Prabhat Printing Press, Delhi.

Preface

The Universal Declaration of Human Rights is a declaration adopted by the United Nations General Assembly on December 10, 1948 at the Palais de Chaillot in Paris. The Declaration has been translated into at least 375 languages and dialects, making it the most widely translated document in the world. The Declaration arose directly from the experience of the Second World War and represents the first global expression of rights to which all human beings are entitled. It consists of 30 articles which have been elaborated in subsequent international treaties, regional human rights instruments, national constitutions and laws. The International Bill of Human Rights consists of the Universal Declaration of Human Rights, the International Covenant on Economic, Social and Cultural Rights and the International Covenant on Civil and Political Rights.

The history of human rights involves religious, cultural, philosophical and legal developments throughout recorded history. While the modern human rights movement hugely expanded in post-World War II era, the concept can be traced through all major religions, cultures and philosophies. Ancient Hindu law, Confucianism, the Qur'an and the Ten Commandments all outline some of the rights now included in the Universal Declaration of Human Rights.

The concept of natural law, guaranteeing natural rights despite varying human laws and customs, can be traced back to Ancient Greek philosophers, while Enlightenment philosophers suggest a social contract between the rulers and the ruled. The world's first Buddhist state in India, known as the Maurya Empire, established the world's first welfare system, including free hospitals and education. The African concept of ubuntu is a cultural view of what it is to be human. Modern human rights thinking is descended from these many traditions of human values and beliefs.

The present book International Law and Human Rights is an in depth-systematized study of recent developments, particularly since 1970s, in the international concern for promotion and protection of basic human rights within and beyond national boundaries. This has been necessitated by tremendous growth and taking place of a good number of international treaties, conventions, declarations and practices which are not noticed in books though these are actually followed by the States, and to varying extent these are enforced by the concerned international, regional or national authorities. In many cases, these developments in favour of human rights for people are now integral part of international law and form part of international diplomacy, international relations or international politics.

The book will also find favour with academics, social activists and all those responsible citizens concerned for international human rights denial or suffering on any account in any section of the society.

Meenakshi Arora

Contents

1

Nature and Scope of International Human Rights

Introduction

Universalist theories of human rights derive from western concepts of natural law originating from the Roman Empire, evolving in face of many challenges through the Renaissance and Enlightenment periods into the contemporary industrial and post-industrial age. Human, as distinct from citizens' or other rights derived from membership of specific communities, are claimed on no other grounds than human identity, and are to be enjoyed equally by everyone. On this basis, Jack Donnelly defines the human rights project as translating rights which everyone has into enjoyment and legal codification of their actual substance. This assumes arrangement of legal and political systems so that human rights are paramount, 'trumping' all other systems of law and administration. Paradoxically, to the extent that this is achieved, consciousness of their universal nature can be lost.

Despite its strong intuitive appeal, natural law is highly problematic as a basis for rights claims, as there is no universally agreed account of human nature, which contains base as well as ethical characteristics. The normative nature of the universal human rights project must, therefore, be frankly acknowledged. Even so, emphasis on *rights* indicates far more than mere aspiration or a morally desirable state of affairs. Rights imply entitlements which everyone must be accorded, whatever their status or situation. The notion of universal entitlement raises questions of obligation since, if everyone has rights, each person has an obligation to ensure their fulfillment. Donnelly asserts that liberal rights theories have historically recognised this nexus, despite characterisations of rampant individualism by critics though he acknowledges their validity in relation to unfettered promotion of property rights in contemporary neo-liberal theory. Donnelly claims that only the liberal-democratic formulation asserts rights as equal, inalienable and intrinsic, as a basis for powerful claims against the state. Obligations derive both from one's own and others' rights. Opposing communitarian formulations, whether of the marxist, corporatist-authoritarian or traditional variety, grant rights on the basis of social roles and performance of duties, as defined by custom or the relevant authorities. Donnelly further claims that, apart from rights to self-determination, UN texts refer overwhelmingly to individual rather than group rights. Though embedded in socio-political contexts, groups such as families essentially act as intermediate social groups protecting individual family members. Therefore, families may not deny freedom of religion, rights of political participation or discriminate on grounds of gender. Acknowledging the inconclusiveness of previous attempts to find either a moral or anthropological account of human nature which would command general consent, he claims that there is nevertheless a 'remarkable international normative consensus', supporting in principle if not in practice the list of rights contained in the International Bill of Rights. Continuing reaffirmation over time serves to de-legitimise violations. However, many Asian leaders reject the basic idea of universality with regard to both meaning and application. Donnelly responds that formulation of rights in these texts should for that reason not be regarded as fixed, but as evolving in relation to changes in technology, society and notions of human dignity. The latter depend on how they are understood within different societies, religions and cultures. While universality cannot be claimed *a priori*, too strenuous attempts to find consensus are likely to result in a lowest common denominator approach. Normative claims can be further asserted in terms of Kant's principle that what ought to be cannot be justified merely by purely anthropological reference to what is, and the consequent need to strive for a 'public law of mankind'. Merely recognising that notions of human dignity can be identified in most, and probably all major world religions, leads only to obligations to respect, as distinct from recognising them as a basis of rights. Key issues in categorising and prioritising rights include:

1. The possibility of extracting core or basic rights from the extensive list of rights in the various UN covenants and conventions;
2. The relationship between so called civil and political as against economic, social and cultural rights.

The idea of a short list of rights which should be regarded as paramount and universal has received support from both western and non-western sources, with even dedicated anti-universalists such as former Singapore Prime Minister, Lee Kuan Yew, supporting outlawing of genocide, torture and racial discrimination. Fouad Ajami adds food security, which he claims as defensible as within state capacities in a context of widespread violations. Cranston implicitly supports the short list concept, with pleas that 'universal, paramount, categorical moral rights' should not be trivialised by marginal claims for paid holidays and similar contingent, often unrealisable rights. However, lack of consensus on core rights is illustrated by Cranston's exclusion of economic and social rights, which he regards as neither universal, practical nor of paramount importance, by contrast with the fundamental nature of rights to life, liberty and property. Conversely, Vincent, argues that only the limited goal of placing subsistence and security against violence, as conditions for all other rights, at the centre of international relations agendas, can have a reasonable prospect of gaining consensus.

Conservatives tend to see 'basic needs' agendas as entailing extensive and undesirable interventions in international markets and management. Acknowledging interdependence will lengthen the list of basic rights. Liberals object that this least common denominator approach will allow power holders discretion to define and limit universal standards, also implying that other human rights are not basic and may be sacrificed as need arises. Vincent counters that 'the international community cannot be as adept in practice at keeping all the human rights balls in the air at once as Donnelly is in theory. The moral simplicity of the case is its merit'. While not postulating suppression of civil liberties as a pre-condition, he anticipates that 'subsistence might make a more workable international programme, a more neutral undertaking for international society, than liberty'.

Despite assertions of 'universality, indivisibility and interdependence' between civil-political and economic-social-cultural rights in official UN pronouncements, re-affirmed in Article 5 of the 1993 Vienna Declaration and Programme of Action (VDPA) by the World Conference on Human Rights, Asian countries claim that unequal status is accorded to each. Historically, both streams of rights are central to the 1948 UDHR and have been woven into all subsequent UN covenants and conventions. They were never intended to be separated. But a false dualism took root as a consequence of the Cold War, de-colonisation processes, and struggles by the Third World for a New International Economic Order (NIEO).

Cranston's distinction between positive and negative rights is used to support western conservatives' refusal to recognise economic and social rights. These are claimed as requiring extensive expenditure and complex policy provision, compared with civil and political rights which only require legislation preventing state interference with the liberties of citizens. In reality, many 'positive' programmes, such as legal education, police training, and establishment of electoral commissions are necessary to ensuring that civil liberties are respected and elections properly conducted. Conversely, state restraint, for example, in not appropriating food producing land for other development purposes may be sufficient to ensure subsistence.

Thus all rights require both positive and negative action for their preservation, with the relative importance of each determined according to context. Even if the distinction is acknowledged, there is no intrinsic reason to favour negative over positive rights, as both serve to counter threats to human dignity. As resources to provide subsistence are almost always available, killing is morally equivalent, whether by positive action or neglect. A liberal conception of human rights thus requires integration between both kinds of rights although, in Donnelly's view, some strands of liberal thought have exaggerated property rights to the extent of distorting overall balance. Issues in achieving integration of rights will be taken up in later discussion of links between democracy, development and human rights.

Universalism and Relativism

The core issue at stake here, reflected in the Asian values debate explored in the next chapter, is between asserting core values and principles of human behaviour, while allowing some contextual variations, or denying universality by accepting that human rights are determined by culture and associated social identity. While national sovereignty, economic development, the individual's role relative to the state, and rejection of links between democracy and economic neo-liberalism feature strongly, it is culture which provides basic support for the relativist position, fuelling attacks on claims to universality as ethnocentric, and as manifestations of cultural imperialism.

Reference to cultural aspects in relevant treaties is fairly thin. Cultural rights are added to economic and social rights, which are spelt out in far greater detail. Cultural rights are mentioned in this appendage form just once in the UDHR. The ICESCR refers only to the right to participate in cultural life, conceived primarily in terms of artistic production and intellectual property rights. Rights to enjoy one's culture are set out in Article 27 of the ICCPR, in the context of minority rights, while Article 18 strongly affirms freedom of religion. A UDHR of Indigenous Peoples has been under consideration for several years. But overall failure to integrate notions of culture into mainstream international human rights theory and practice partly explains the sense of distance and lack of ownership which many non-western participants display towards notions of universality claimed for UN instruments.

Prospects for dialogue, leading to either reconciliation between relativist and universalist viewpoints or some more inclusive form of universality, have been widely canvassed. But general consent to the 1993 Vienna Declaration formula of universality with contextual variations did not prevent continuing attacks on the legitimacy of universal human rights. Acceptance, even in principle, to undertake dialogue over their nature and content is proving equally problematic. Liberals urge that communitarian and liberal standpoints are irreconcilably opposed, and attempts at syncretism will result in either a 'lowest common denominator' outcome, or the incorporation of mutually antagonistic values.

Others see dialogue as essential to human understanding, even if only to agree to disagree as part of a search for a more peaceful and prosperous world. Camilleri suggests that dialogue may reveal that competing claims of universalism and cultural relativism may prove less contradictory than often assumed. Comparison between distinct religious or ethical traditions can yield universal standards, so long as these are not interpreted as immutable or absolute. To be credible, universalism must be deeply embedded within each culture, requiring a dynamic, ongoing process of interaction, dialogue and re-negotiation. Thus it is possible to extract values of respect for the dignity of life, linked to notions of humane and legitimate governance from the four major non-western religions - Islam, Hinduism, Buddhism and Confucianism. Differences with western traditions, it is claimed, are more of form and emphasis.

Vincent is more doubtful of finding common ground across cultures, since it is equally possible to identify differences as similarities. The exercise may nevertheless prove useful in encouraging people to articulate their values, thereby providing data bases for identifying potential commonalities. Implicitly, such attempts assume some measure of universalism, in accepting that cross-cultural explorations are not precluded by cultural relativism. Moreover, they can easily end up merely recording variety and allowing groups to pick and choose.

Third World countries also appeal to universal values, for example, in asserting racial equality, claiming rights to self-determination and development. Nor are they willing to grant the West immunity from criticism entailed by total cultural relativism. Major world religions all claim universal validity in varying degrees. However, there is no way, in culturally relative terms, to argue against assertions of superiority by one culture or religion over another. Consequently, in the search for at least minimum international standards of justice, surrender to what John Stuart Mill described as the 'despotism of custom' can only be avoided by the procedure of fully testing what is right through debate, and taking necessary action.

National Sovereignty and International Human Rights Law

The notion of universal human rights poses a fundamental challenge to the rationale underlying state sovereignty, by which states are autonomous both in exercising jurisdiction within their territorial boundaries and pursuing their national interest in conducting external affairs. States jealously safeguard, and the international system formally upholds the principle of state sovereignty. Nevertheless, state claims for immunity from external scrutiny are becoming increasingly unsustainable, as are claims for non-intervention against conduct that threatens general stability or outrages the conscience of humanity.

States' capacity to behave autonomously varies greatly according to their relative strength *vis a vis* other states and transnational actors. According to the 'realist' view, states are the sole bearers of rights and responsibilities in international society. Individuals can only access that society through the agency of states and are objects not subjects of international law. However, international human rights law refers extensively to the rights of individuals. Human rights treaties bind those states which have ratified them, to the extent they have not entered reservations, while membership of the UN entails at least formal acceptance of the UDHR.

Human rights discourse in international relations contexts has tended to assume polarity between realism and idealism. At one extreme are those who assert that the world community consists only of states. At the other are those who see a cosmopolitan community of individuals, which alone can shape political groupings or systems. A third group dismisses entirely talk of a world community and associated human rights as a misnomer concealing vested interests. Within western traditions, realist challenges to ideas of rights have been mounted by conservatives such as Edmund Burke, espousing the virtues of tradition, hierarchy, mutual affection, duty and obligation; utilitarians such as Jeremy Bentham, who described pursuit of abstract rights, as distinct from real rights deriving from government and society, as 'nonsense on stilts'; organic state theorists, such as Hegel who contends that the individual's ethical existence only finds expression in national community, from which all laws, rights and duties derive; and Marx, who characterises liberal notions of rights as based solely on class interest.

Parallels are apparent between organic state theory and the communitarian cum corporatist ideology and political practice of several Southeast Asian states. Hegel's notion that the nation-state has its own personality, with positive rights to assert its existence, fits well with assertions of individual subordination to the collectivity. However, according to Vincent, ideas of rights based on a universal moral order are proving resilient in the face of these challenges, with contemporary philosophers ranging from Nozik to Rawls returning to pre-eighteenth century natural law concepts. In practice, the 'individual versus community' puzzle can be worked out via standard democratic 'rule of law' formulations. At the same time, one powerful consequence from Marx's challenge has been to spawn a host of new economic and social rights.

De Vries cites three major strands to realist attacks on the role of moral norms in international politics. First, there is no agreed international code of morality. This is ascribed by Hans Morgenthau to the absence of any integrated international society capable of defining the concrete meaning of justice or equality, as in national societies. Secondly, this reality reflects the truth in Thomas Hobbes' extreme dictum that there is neither morality nor law outside the state, so that international anarchy, competition and lack of trust between states necessitates a primary emphasis on survival. While states are not as weak as individuals, and the 'golden rule' of behaving to others as you would wish them to behave to yourself is very relevant to survival, conflict cannot always be avoided. Finally, the ethic of responsibility which this situation imposes on power holders is concerned primarily with outcomes rather than moral qualities or intentions.

K.W. Thompson argues that the equation of realism with amorality is unfair, evidenced by the concern with issues of morality by distinguished scholars of this school, such as Morgenthau and Niebuhr. Thompson sees the core of realist thinking as a rejection of absolutist views of right and wrong, in which demands for rights are often not linked to acknowledgement of responsibilities for the consequences of actions demanded. Utopians, Thompson claims, assume unilinear progress, a moulding of the 'new man' in which self-interest and power balances become obsolete. In that context, moral self-righteousness sees no need for external rules or constraints. A more balanced approach is to gradually build up a sense of international community through networks of overlapping programmes as a basis for evolving international law and government. Traditional diplomacy has a vital role to play here.

Donnelly agrees that realists do not reject notions of morality in world affairs, but considers they are unable to see any way to integrate it with the reality of the states system. Given their view that international politics is a struggle between power-maximising states in an environment of anarchy, those failing to maximise power leave themselves open to attack. According to this equation, it is a dangerous mistake to use human rights for any purpose other than furthering national interest. But even if this is conceded as the cardinal principle of foreign policy, there is no reason why human rights should be excluded more than other aspects with potential for conflict, such as trade, investment, resources or the environment. States pursue a full range of policy instruments in such matters, including persuasion, incentives, diplomatic signals and, in extreme cases, sanctions or the use of force. *Prima facie*, these are as legitimate for human rights as for other policy goals. Therefore, while sovereignty is the starting point, it is not necessarily the end point of international law.

Vincent argues that there is no reason why human rights should lead to the destruction of the states system of international relations. Indeed, human rights can add to states' legitimacy, while their absence over time has the reverse effect. In practice, states have a history of co-opting and translating human rights into citizens' rights, gradually integrating them into daily dealings between states. To the extent that this is true, it fulfils Donnelly's paradox by which adopting the content of human rights will cause their universal aspects to become obscured. Such a process might even calm the soul of Edmund Burke, who was fond of contrasting the concrete and 'ancient liberties of England' with the abstract 'rights of man'.

Less reassuring to conservatives, as well as neo-liberals, is Vincent's claim that state power and authority have expanded rapidly with the growth in human rights ideology. While concentrations of state power have occurred for many other reasons, human rights agendas certainly require extensive legislation and expenditure by governments. Fears of a more active state, and by extension UN-linked international institutions, may well be at the heart of conservative opposition to universal human rights, with dismissals of them as utopian more in the nature of a pretext.

UN Human Rights Regimes and The States System

International human rights law, embedded in UN covenants and conventions, co-exists in constant tension with principles of national sovereignty. At base, UN structures and processes reflect the states' system, operating as a permanent forum and clearing house for transactions between them. Membership consists exclusively of sovereign states, which collectively exercise voting rights and decision-making powers. But as most states are unwilling to accept adverse decisions, negotiation and application of agreements is mainly conducted outside the institutional framework of the UN.

Implementation of human rights regimes is coordinated by the UNCHR, which was established as a Functional Commission of the UN Economic and Social Council (ECOSOC), to which it continues to report. Specialised treaty committees have developed as sub-commissions of the UNCHR to monitor covenants and conventions. Special rapporteurs may be appointed to investigate persistent violations either in particular countries, or thematically, in areas such as torture across countries.

All states are deemed, by virtue of UN membership, to be bound by the UDHR - a situation prompting some, particularly Asian states to call for its review. But the UDHR is not strictly speaking a treaty, and is, therefore, not binding under international law, despite its great moral force. Although some jurists argue that the UDHR enjoys the status of international customary law, this essentially western concept is looked on with suspicion by many developing countries.

Covenants and conventions, which have the force of treaties, become open for signature and ratification by states following adoption by a majority of the General Assembly. Signature indicates in principle intention to participate. The decisive step of ratification requires states to bring their domestic legal, political and administrative practices into conformity with the relevant treaty. This comes into force once ratified by the requisite number of states specified in the text. Other states may subsequently accede under the same conditions. Ratification or accession entails agreement both to report regularly and submit to Commission investigations.

Several means are open for states to legally limit their responsibility within the treaty process. Limitations to enjoyment of rights may be indicated as part of treaty texts. Thus Article 19(3) of the ICCPR places limits on rights to freedom of expression asserted in Article 19(2) in terms of protecting the rights or reputations of others, national security, public order, public health or morals. Such provisos potentially legitimise sweeping restrictions on civil rights.

Ratifying states may indicate reservations to their acceptance or declare their own interpretations or understandings of particular clauses. Other states may choose whether to accept these, but silence is assumed to signify consent. Under provisions for derogation, Article 4 of the ICCPR allows states, when declaring states of national emergency, to suspend certain human rights provisions, except for rights to life, freedom from torture and slavery, freedom of thought, conscience and religion. Such restrictions must be non-discriminatory and proportional to the situation, which must genuinely threaten the life of the nation. To limit scope for abuse, special rapporteurs are appointed to monitor derogations.

Although the UNCHR lacks powers of its own to enforce treaties, its comprehensive monitoring and reporting process provides a framework for both international and domestic opinion to exert pressures, which may ultimately alter the practice of offending countries. The open and public nature of this process is much feared and resented by some governments, which commonly defend themselves by invoking principles of sovereignty and non-intervention.

States' monopoly over UNCHR processes is limited by three important provisions. Firstly, Resolution 1503 procedure enables individuals or groups to report evidence of a consistent pattern of serious violations within a given state. Secondly, inter-governmental or non-government organisations with permanent observer status at the General Assembly, registered with ECOSOC or invited to attend by the Commission may submit agenda items, speak and tender written submissions at its meetings, but without voting rights. However, a two-thirds majority of members present and voting is required for an item to be included on the agenda. Finally, the First Optional Protocol to the ICCPR, adopted in December 1966, allows individuals to appeal against alleged violations of that Covenant, providing they have exhausted all domestic remedies. This procedure has been extended to CEDAW and is under active consideration for other instruments.

States' submission to these regimes is voluntary. Ratification is the essential first step, indicating states' willingness to open their processes to outside scrutiny, subjecting themselves to international law on an equal footing with others. To be effective, UN human rights regimes require near universal ratification of core instruments, a minimum of reservations, full compliance with reporting and monitoring requirements and willingness to abide by umpires' decisions. While these goals are a long way from achievement, participation in UNCHR reporting and monitoring networks increased significantly during the 1990s, partly boosted by increased UN membership. The range of new instruments in the process of development is also expanding. Significant institutionalisation and deepening of the UN process has potential to change the overall diplomatic environment and ultimately domestic processes in ways favourable to human rights. This prospect is strengthened by the establishment of national human rights institutions and the spread of human rights education through UN affiliated and other informal non-government organisation (NGO) networks. However, excessive bureaucratisation can threaten slowdown and even reversal of such gains.

Humanitarian Intervention

The question of humanitarian intervention against non-complying states, whatever their treaty participation status, is never far from the surface in human rights debates. Unfortunately, advocates of intervention tend to look outside UN processes, due to the perceived impossibility of gaining consensus from member states, and veto powers held by the five permanent Security Council members. The practicality and legitimacy of external intervention mostly flounders on the rock of states' sovereignty. This principle is upheld within the UN Charter and vigorously defended by member states wherever their own interests are involved. It is espoused with particular strength by post-colonial states in Asia, Africa and Latin America.

Military intervention is rarely agreed under UN auspices. Even mass killings bordering on genocide, with conflict posing a threat to regional security, as in Cambodia and East Timor, will not prompt intervention without agreement from all parties. Alternatively, as in Bosnia and Kosovo, western military action may subsequently be legitimised through the UN. In the case of Iraq's invasion of Kuwait, where major powers' interests were at stake, some random human rights protection of minorities may have occurred as a by-product of UN approved intervention. However, subsequent sanctions against Iraq have substantially destroyed the economic rights of its people.

Economic sanctions have never been universally supported, even in the extreme case of South Africa under apartheid. Western attempts to combine economic and diplomatic pressures on Myanmar's military junta rulers have been opposed by China and ASEAN. Policies of linking economic aid to human rights performance command some support in donor countries, but are also resisted on grounds of national sovereignty, as unwisely diluting social and economic disbursement criteria, and as downgrading rights to development relative to civil and political rights. Other types of intervention include low levels of diplomatic protest, advocacy or dialogue, information gathering and dissemination by human rights NGOs, and media coverage. Controversy becomes most intense over measures which impinge on the accused country's domestic politics and administration.

Claims to absolute state autonomy are no longer sustainable, and bases for coexistence and cooperation between states must be continually re-negotiated in an increasingly interdependent world. Difficulties in devising modes of intervention which are legitimate, proportional and not counter-productive to stated objectives rule out any general licence to intervene, with a presumption against all but its least coercive forms under most circumstances. Primary initiative for change must, therefore, continue to rest with states' domestic institutions and processes. But UN human rights regimes can play a legitimate and significant role in exposing states' regimes to scrutiny by their peers. They also provide supporting frameworks for cooperation between domestic and outside groups in achieving change.

Globalisation and Human Rights

Globalisation has a mixed impact on human rights. Its discourse contains many conflicting accounts and ideology-based agendas for global management. David Held emphasises pervasive interconnectedness, evidenced in ever more prolific flows of information, ideas, pollutants, drugs, goods, capital, weapons and knowledge across national boundaries. These increase disjunctions between national identity and the globalisation of culture, with potential to develop a sense of global belonging, challenging or transcending national loyalties. Such trends challenge doctrines that international law is exclusively a matter between states, and generate alternative proposals for organising world order.

The UN Charter, reflecting a desire to outlaw extreme forms of violence against humanity following World War II, fundamentally challenged doctrines of absolute state sovereignty assumed in the 'Westphalian' model of international relations and law. The Charter model includes a rival source of international law, in which (i) people as well as states are subjects of international law; (ii) majority voting in principle overrides consent of individual states. However, constraints such as the Security Council veto and lack of funding have prevented any fundamental break with the logic of the Westphalian system. The UN system, therefore, remains vulnerable to individual state agendas. Even so, it is useful as a forum for seeking solutions to international problems, in which states are at least formally equal. It also has potential as a 'supra-national presence in world affairs championing human rights'. According to Bull, international human rights law potentially subverts state sovereignty insofar as the rights and duties of a person can be proclaimed irrespective of membership of a state. But although profoundly challenged by globalisation, the nation-state 'continues to command loyalty, both as an idea and as an institution'.

According to Falk, states are being by-passed and their legitimacy eroded both by globalising trends beyond their grasp, and by pressures leading to internal fragmentation. This situation is characterised by numerous quasi-government and non-government associations, interests and affiliations crossing national boundaries and jurisdictions, with ethnicity and religion as potent forces in both domestic and international contexts. However, it is premature to expect that the role of states and potency of national sovereignty as an ideological force and focus of popular loyalty will be significantly downgraded in the near future.

Marc Williams claims that theories stressing global interdependence confuse sovereignty with autonomy. States have never been able to exercise absolute control or implement all rights claimed, exercise of which has always been subject to negotiation and relative strength. Interdependence theories tend to concentrate on economic trends, where governments appear to act as spectators to international transactions over which they have little direct control. But states' legal and administrative powers necessitate their cooperation in consolidating property transfers and overall market operations. Consensus or majority decision-making processes, essential to the operation of regional and international bodies, still require the exercise of sovereignty. It is ultimately unclear whether globalisation will be based on continuing national sovereignty, or whether new global structures will transcend the state. While the old internal-external distinctions are becoming less salient, states remain active participants in forging new arrangements. In a word, the exercise of sovereignty is flexible, and has withstood many challenges.

More disorderly outcomes are possible. Rather than replacing the state with a homogeneous global order, globalisation may result in splintering the existing political order. This will have negative outcomes for democratic processes as people's aspirations still focus on their own states' institutions, while the real sites of decision-making are diffused. Systems of control and accountability will become more remote as multilateral regimes accumulate legal powers.

Universal human rights protagonists face major strategic and tactical challenges relating to the future of the states system. It is necessary both to improve ways of integrating human rights within the existing system of sovereign states, and anticipate and adapt to changes resulting from globalisation processes. The human rights implications of any too rapid erosion of state sovereignty, whether legally or *de facto*, are also uncertain and will depend crucially on which global governance models ultimately prevail.

Falk identifies two general paradigms, which he labels as geo- and humane governance. By 'geo-governance' is meant reliance on traditional power politics approaches, elite arrangements between leading players, by-passing or neutralising national governments and such democratic processes as they variously possess. While asserting principles of national sovereignty, the national interests of dominant states, particularly the United States of America (USA), determine overall strategies. Systems of 'inhumane governance' pursued under conventional paths to globalisation stand accused under a 'triple indictment' of causing global apartheid, through divisions within a partly race-based system divided into rich and poor worlds, avoidable harm through militarisation and eco-imperialism processes, causing massive destruction to both the natural environment and people's subsistence systems.

By contrast, 'humane governance' focuses on people-centred goals such as peace, food and a clean environment. In human rights terms this requires comprehensive approaches embracing the full spectrum of civil, political, economic, social and cultural rights, linked to systems of democratic order and security capable of supporting them, including major reforms of the UN.

Humane governance paradigms commonly oppose notions of democracy based on unqualified systems of majoritarianism, which may marginalise rights of women and minorities or aggravate racial, ethnic and religious tensions. Globalisation, by creating new forms of civil society, opens up possibilities for extending democratisation movements beyond state-society relations to all arenas of power and authority - corporations, banks, workplaces, and even to personal relationships, as home and society are often the source of non-humane cultural values.

Humane governance models are ambivalent towards national sovereignty. On the one hand, self-determination rights are espoused both by recently independent states and by national minorities seeking sovereignty. The interests of these two groupings frequently conflict in the Asian region and elsewhere. Conversely, strong nationalist assertions, especially those based on ethnic or racial identity, frequently undermine both minority rights and democratic processes. Sovereignty is also routinely invoked to resist external criticism of militarisation and environmental destruction within territorial boundaries. Yet it remains important in resisting intervention by powerful states. Even some north European states, as adherents of welfare capitalism, continue to be effective agents for realising economic and social rights, though increasingly challenged by global market forces.

In most developing countries, claims on citizens, based on territorial community, override individual rights. But globalisation is breaking down monopolies of political loyalty and authority, with new trans-territorial forms of association and identity competing, in turn provoking various backlashes aimed at coercing conformity to states' cultural norms. The continuing reality of sovereignty and mixed consequences of these conflicting trends must be accepted by those seeking paths to humane governance.

Democracy, Development and Human Rights

Article 8 of the United Nations VDPA states that 'Democracy, development and respect for human rights and fundamental freedoms are interdependent and mutually reinforcing' and calls on the international community to strengthen and promote all three equally. Subsequent chapters will draw out regional and local understandings of this triangular relationship, which lies at the heart of Southeast Asian human rights debates.

Democracy and Human Rights

Democracy and human rights are distinct but related concepts. Links between them are both mutually supportive and conflicting. While democratic forms of government can be conceived as a major, indeed essential means for achieving human rights, minority rights can be overridden by majority will. Elected governments can entrench their position by sweeping national security legislation restricting freedom of expression and association.

Developing countries urge that both human rights and democracy are open to localised understandings and applications. Nevertheless, Articles 21 of the UDHR and 25 of the ICCPR assert equal rights of citizens to take part in the conduct of public affairs, directly or through freely chosen representatives; to vote and be elected at 'genuine periodic elections' based on universal and equal suffrage, secret ballot, guaranteeing the free expression and will of the electors. Coupled with other rights to freedom of speech, association and peaceful assembly, and allowing for variation in electoral and constitutional arrangements, little scope remains, on the basis of UN human rights law, for legitimising 'Asian', 'people's', 'guided' or other adjectivally qualified forms of democracy.

Even so, inclusion of democratic ground rules, commonly described as 'liberal', within the overall framework of international human rights law does not equate to the totality of human rights, which embraces economic and social as well as civil and political rights. Both the content of these rights and the means of achieving them are major objects of democratic contestation. This is implicitly acknowledged by some neo-liberals, such as Hayek, who sees liberalism as a doctrine about what law ought to be, whereas democracy is a doctrine about how to determine the law. Individuals require rules constraining governments and majorities, freeing them from fear of coercive power. Otherwise, neo-liberal protagonists must persuade majorities to their viewpoint. Huntington similarly defines democracy in terms of law and process.

Such minimalist conceptions of democracy have potential merit in undercutting tendencies by both radicals and neo-liberals to define democracy in programmatic terms, labelling disfavoured outcomes from political competition as undemocratic. However, limited focus on democratic competition processes and associated legal rights ignores the impact of globalisation in shifting the loci of decision-making away from national governments and legislatures.

In response, new movements and concepts of democratic governance have emerged transcending national boundaries, expressed in terms such as 'international cosmopolitan democracy' and 'humane governance'. Neo-liberals have attempted to depict economic and social rights asserted in UN covenants as merely undesirable objects of democratic contestation rather than as fundamental rights. Gill claims that neo-liberals have sought by various legal and constitutional devices to privilege rights of capital and entrench disciplines of the world market place beyond the control of democratic politics. Thus, a merely legal and procedural view of democracy may be instrumental in denying human rights. Conversely, constitutionally entrenching every kind of right would represent a limitation on democratic processes, as conventionally defined.

In order to develop participatory structures appropriate to emerging sites of contestation, it is necessary to transcend traditional boundaries between domestic and international politics. Held identifies seven such sites, arguing that asymmetrical power balances in any of them diminish people's life chances, autonomy and participatory possibilities. These relate to physical and emotional wellbeing in terms of health, nutrition and shelter; access to goods and services sufficient to avoid 'poverty traps'; opportunities for enjoyment of cultural life, free from constraints imposed by state, religious authorities, or other hegemonic groups within civil society; access to and control of civic associations; economic life and associated structures of production, distribution and exchange, consumption and social class; the domain of security, violence and other forms of coercive relations, embracing both state and para-state forces and insurgent groups; intra-state legal and inter-state regulatory institutions and networks.

Held considers conventional civil and political rights approaches insufficient to ensure application of what he calls democratic public law in all the above spheres.

This requires establishment of clear rights and obligations pertinent to all spheres of power. Evolution in this direction ultimately requires a strong cluster of democratic states and societies. Sustainability of democratic systems within individual states requires deepening and strengthening of 'international cosmopolitan democracy', applying principles of subsidiarity in determining sites of decision-making appropriate to the context and range of interconnectedness entailed.

While such agendas apparently fly in the face of an international system still largely based on state sovereignty, the case for viewing states' international legitimacy as linked to upholding common democratic values is implicit in UDHR Articles 21 and ICCPR Article 25 cited earlier, and explicit in UDHR Article 28, which asserts that 'everyone is entitled to a social and international order in which the rights and freedoms set forth in this Declaration can be fully realized.' The Council of Europe makes commitment to democracy a condition of membership, while the European Convention on Human Rights explicitly links them. The Declaration of the 1992 Helsinki Conference on Security and Cooperation in Europe also signed by Canada and the USA views human rights as matters of direct and legitimate concern to all participatory states, and not exclusively within the domain of the state concerned. Promoting human rights and strengthening democratic institutions is integral to building comprehensive security in Europe (Held 1995:105). Paradoxically, the international order is increasingly structured by agencies over which citizens have minimal control, at the very time when popular democratic demands are becoming more assertive.

The humane governance school is similarly global in its outlook. However, it is 'hawkish' towards liberal notions of democracy and any hint of special privileging of civil and political rights. In a critique which indicates partial incorporation of communitarian ideas into humane governance models, Falk advocates a system of democracy which is concrete and contextualised, emphasising the locus of authority and distribution of benefits in class, gender, and ethnic terms. While conceding some value to traditional democratic forms as protecting citizens against the state and facilitating a measure of popular participation in selecting leaders, they are seen as unable to provide humane governance in face of relentless pressures to assert the primacy of market principles over welfare, social harmony and environmental protection and even minimal democratic rights.

Humane governance advocates, see a strong transnational social movement as essential to changing this situation. This idea is reflected in a blueprint proposing to institutionalise representation and consultation of NGOs and civil society groups in a reformed UN structure. Although this idea is intended to complement rather than replace representation by states, it highlights sharply competing principles of representation. NGOs are mostly unelected, tending rather to play intermediary roles in promoting grassroots empowerment. Their links with local members or reference groups become increasingly indirect as they scale up their engagement at national and international levels.

State and Civil Society

Despite the relative weakness of civil society in most Southeast Asian states, a wide range of advocacy groups and associations have emerged among women, peasants, workers, landless, ethnic minorities, environmental and human rights groups, supported by sympathetic journalists, lawyers and other professionals. They have mostly shown greater capacity to bring their case to wider audiences and gain attention from policy-makers compared with weak, divided and often semi-legal opposition parties. But their future relations with political parties in more fully developed systems of electoral democracy will be more complex than currently acknowledged in their public rhetoric.

The examples of India and the Philippines indicate sharp and often bitter rivalry with politicians. NGOs and advocacy groups maintain popular legitimacy to the extent that they do not seek power for themselves. When politicians point to such groups' lack of electoral legitimacy, they commonly respond by denouncing money politics and 'the system' in general. As yet there is little consensus concerning division of labour among those seeking democratic change, and reconciling electoral-style representation with more direct, popular forms of participation.

The beneficial impact on many disadvantaged groups need not entail undifferentiated support for strengthening civil society as uniquely representing the forces of good against oppressive governments, as in some radical cum populist rhetoric. Religious and ethnic sentiment can be easily incited and manipulated in times of crisis, indicating a need for cooperative action between state and non-state groups in developing a civic culture supportive of democratic values and practices.

Fine and Rai urge moving away from polarised perspectives on civil society, and the need to include those who can currently find no place in its associational life. In terms of humane governance objectives, governments may at times serve as vehicles of moderation in relation to regressive populism. Cultural rights are also not unlimited and must be linked to a culture of democratic toleration.

Despite these qualifications, normative and practical convergences between democratic movements and efforts to strengthen civil society relative to the state remain strong. Trends towards incorporating community groups into state structures have placed a premium on forming independent associations with some real measure of autonomy. This entails challenging communitarian ideology designed to suppress individual rights. But equally, non-state groups need not necessarily accept standard liberal pluralist models which construct them as mere interest groups or intermediaries, and may choose to play more broad-ranging community building and identity forming roles.

Relations between governments and NGOs are subject to many strains and contradictions. Elements within governments, particularly those concerned with delivering economic and social development programmes, appreciate the need for some measure of popular participation, and seek cooperation with NGOs for this purpose. Foreign aid donors also impose conditionalities favouring community input. Although governments fear that popular mobilisation will challenge its authority, heavy-handed control will undermine NGOs' popular legitimacy and effectiveness. For their part, NGOs recognise that scattered localised successes will not make any large-scale impact without engagement with macro-political processes. Cooperation with government agencies helps them gain access to resources and opportunities to influence policy and planning in more participatory directions. But these gains must be weighed against ever present dangers of losing autonomy.

Development and Human Rights

The UN Declaration on the Right to Development (RTD) adopted by the General Assembly on 4 December 1986 brought together developing country aspirations for national development in a sharper, more focused way compared with the ICESCR. The language of rights is sustained throughout the document in terms of the full range of human rights set out in UN covenants and conventions. Article 2(1) asserts the human person as the central subject of development, as both active participant and beneficiary.

While the Declaration gives states important rights and responsibilities, nothing in its content supports interpretations of development in purely economic terms or related insistence by some governments that its achievement must precede adoption of civil and political rights. Indeed, Article 6(3) sees their absence as an obstacle to development which states are urged to eliminate. The Preamble asserts that 'the promotion of, respect for and enjoyment of certain human rights and fundamental freedoms cannot justify the denial of other human rights and fundamental freedoms.' Article 9(2) provides that nothing in the Declaration justifies violation of rights set out in the UDHR or associated covenants and conventions.

The RTD Declaration nevertheless accommodates developing country government concerns in important ways. States are acknowledged as having both a right and a duty to formulate national development plans designed to enhance the welfare of all their people. Article 2(2) asserts individuals' rights to participate in planning processes and enjoy a fair distribution of resulting benefits. But they must also accept responsibility for development and their duties to the community as corollaries to enjoying respect for their human rights. Articles 3 and 4 require protection of these rights to be matched by international cooperation to establish a 'new international economic order', and promote more rapid development in poorer countries.

Article 5 calls for resolute steps to eliminate the 'massive and flagrant violations' of human rights resulting from apartheid, racial discrimination, colonialism, foreign domination and occupation, aggression, threats against national sovereignty, unity and territorial integrity, threats of war and refusal to recognise fundamental rights to self-determination. Later articles deal with peace and security, access to basic resources in terms of education, health services, food, housing, employment and the fair distribution of income, including effective measures to ensure that women participate equally in both the processes and benefits of development.

While it is easy to dismiss the Declaration as a pious wish list, offering something to all main protagonists in north-south conflicts, it represents a potentially important step in linking human rights and development agendas, re-affirming principles of indivisibility. But the opportunity which the RTD Declaration offered was not taken up. This was partly due to unfavourable timing, with neo-liberal ideology dominating the thinking of key western countries, and international institutions such as the International Monetary Fund (IMF) and the World Bank. Proposals for a New International Economic Order (NIEO), which would have changed the ground rules for conducting aid, trade, commodity pricing technology transfer, investment and other areas of vital economic concern to developing countries, were similarly rejected. The NIEO's residual Keynesian outlook, favouring mixed economies and government initiative, was similarly unacceptable to international decision makers, who insisted on their own structural adjustment agendas.

Despite some softening in this outlook in the latter part of the 1990s, particularly in light of the Asian economic crisis, there is still underlying reluctance by richer countries to accord either development, or economic and social rights generally, full status as human *rights*, as distinct from desirable objectives. The roots of such reluctance are both legal and political, based on fears that poorer countries will gain open-ended claims on rich country resources. Goals, means and indicators of development are in any case hotly disputed. Consequently, neither definitions nor principles for enforcement can be agreed. India's Constitution implicitly recognises the problem, distinguishing between 'fundamental rights', broadly corresponding to civil and political rights, and economic and social objectives, accorded priority as 'directive principles'. Only the former are justiciable.

While neo-liberals find little support in either the RTD or ICESCR document, parts of the RTD find resonance with developing countries pursuing conventional growth policies but frustrated by external pressures for privatisation, de-regulation and conditionalities imposed on aid, trade and investment, in what they see as an unequally structured global order. Some governments assert developmental rights in international contexts, while repressing them at home, fearing their use by civil society groups to promote participatory and basic needs oriented approaches.

Attempts to entrench indivisibility principles in economic and social planning and overall systems of governance, under the general rubric of a 'right to development', are gaining some momentum. Preambles to the UDHR, ICCPR and ICESCR requiring state parties to respect, protect and promote human rights, justify shifting the onus on governments from moral and humanitarian to legal obligation.

The Human Rights Council of Australia, as part of a like-minded international network, has sought to systematise these requirements by developing a 'Rights Way to Development' Manual. Though focusing primarily on external aid policy and practice, its approach links UN treaties and reporting networks, national human rights plans and relevant domestic institutions. The model entails spelling out the implications of each right for corresponding areas of national policy, together with specific sectoral targets.

Many NGOs, including those advocating popular empowerment, are ambivalent about rights-based approaches. While welcoming the shift towards equity-based claims, they sense that one-dimensional legal approaches will prove inadequate and even counter-productive without social, cultural and institutional change. They also fear that externally imposed formulae may weaken participatory objectives, central to their ethos and legitimacy.

Attempts to develop operational models and checklists aimed at integrating UN covenant rights within a framework of overall strategic plans nevertheless provide bases for performance monitoring and application of pressure where appropriate. They further help to concretise human rights discourse and legitimise a praxis of mutual accountability and peer pressure, while the focus on development assistance obligations in RTD blueprints helps redress perceived imbalances in global protection and promotion of human rights.

Post-colonial countries have commonly promoted states as prime agents of development. While earlier notions of public sector dominated planning have been modified or abandoned, with dynamic private sectors emerging in East and Southeast Asia, the legitimacy and need for governments to play pro-active roles represents a strong point of convergence between otherwise diverse states. Active partnership between government and business, culturally underpinned by values of cooperation and harmony, is also extolled. This outlook is challenged by both neo-liberals and advocates of strengthened civil society roles, who see it as promoting patronage, corruption and inefficiency. Asian values rhetoric thus partly represents a form of covert resistance to anti-statist economic ideology, in which it is more politic to denounce liberal democratic understandings of human rights than to openly attack powerful 'sacred cows' of free markets, de-regulation and privatisation.

As Falk has pointed out, there is no necessary correlation between economic efficiency and democracy, with hegemonic powers swinging from support for authoritarian regimes pursuing market-oriented policies to post-Cold War demands for democratisation as necessary to good governance. The paradox is apparently explained by the legitimacy and 'rule of law' which democracy is expected to bring, despite potential for social disorder in the shorter term.

Clarifying the future role of governments is vital to determining strategies for promoting economic and social rights. If life is to be governed overwhelmingly by the interplay of market forces, such rights could become very marginalised, although there will always be a residual role for both state and civil society in regulating rules of engagement and balancing outcomes to disadvantaged groups. According to Cerny, while a core role remains for the state, its holistic and overarching character is giving way to a plurality of structures and processes providing public goods. Pressures for states to be competitive push them increasingly in the enterprise association direction, while abandoning or downgrading traditional roles.

Linda Weiss argues that this trend is not inevitable, with neo-liberal policies as much the outcome of ideological choice as of dominance of international capital. States' alleged powerlessness in face of globalising trends serves as a convenient tool for marketing unpopular policies. In reality, states play wide-ranging initiating, capacity-building and adaptive roles in many domestic, regional and international contexts. Some operate as major vehicles of capital accumulation, as in the case of Singapore, which Weiss claims as maintaining active control over its savings and investment levels.

The government-business partnership, Weiss claims, goes to the heart of state capacity. By contrast, Anglo-American economies, including Australia, with their traditional 'arms length' approach to the corporate sector, lack the strategic capacities of their East Asian counterparts, so that the fundamentals of these coordinated economies remain strong despite the post-1997 currency crisis. Though the crisis generated increased scepticism towards East Asian development models, the inadequacies of neo-liberal alternatives were also exposed. Weiss' analysis goes far in explaining both the core rationale underlying regional resistance to western neo-liberal pressures and the lack of convergence between regional approaches and the major thrust of UN Right to Development and related economic human rights agendas.

Summary

UN treaty processes offer significant scope for interpretation and harmonisation with domestic norms and practices, monitoring and reporting processes place an onus on participating states to explain and justify their position, thereby instituting formal frameworks for mutual accountability.

While the right to enter reservations preserves national sovereignty, other countries retain rights to criticise and even reject arguments framed in terms of domestic law and practice, where these contravene UN treaty objectives. Such arrangements formally refute doctrines that states' internal affairs are beyond external comment. However, treaty accountability requirements, and the opportunities they offer to critics at home and abroad to highlight deficiencies continue to discourage states' participation. As China and the USA still refuse to ratify major covenants and conventions, many issues bearing on human rights are sidelined or resolved outside UN frameworks.

This chapter has highlighted links between debates concerning the relative or universal nature of human rights, reconciling principles of national sovereignty and international human rights law, and practical and philosophical problems of integrating the two major streams of human rights. While UN doctrine strongly asserts the interdependence of all human rights, definitions and causal links between democracy, development and human rights are complex and strongly contested. Resolution of this triangular equation lies at the heart of human rights struggles and discourse, both globally and in Southeast Asia.

2

Democracy and Development of Human Rights in Asia

Introduction

Historically, western governments have tended to accept local conditions as a basis for policy-making, subject to economic and strategic interests and despite intermittent enthusiasm for imposing 'enlightenment'. This outlook persisted into the post-colonial era, according with requirements of diplomatic protocol and pragmatism. Imperatives of political stability during the Cold War period consolidated this approach, which was intellectually reinforced by realist schools of thought in the fields of international relations and Third World development politics. But the balance of forces favouring this approach has been upset both within western democracies and Southeast Asia since the end of the Cold War, encouraging stronger impulses towards democratisation and placing human rights issues firmly on global and regional agendas.

The sudden outpouring of Asian values polemic in the early 1990s was in part a defensive reaction against mounting pressures for political liberalisation and conformity with international human rights standards. Widespread acknowledgement of their economic success added to regional governments' sense of vindication and grievance towards changing trends. But Asian values discourse also represented a conscious attempt to draw together common elements from diverse cultural strands into a coherent alternative concept of politics and society. While legitimising regime dominance, appeals to national and cultural pride also enjoy a measure of popular resonance. Such themes have antecedents in earlier decolonisation struggles and Third World demands for an NIEO.

Singapore and Malaysia have led the way in articulating contemporary Asian values concepts. The best known version emerged from the response by Kishore Mahbubani, an influential member of Singapore's policy-making elite, to Samuel Huntington's 'Clash of Civilisations' thesis. Mahbubani expressed both his country's concerns over US regional policies and latent frustrations of regional neighbours. Malaysia, angered by US opposition to its East Asian Economic Caucus (EAEC) plan, asserted Third World grievances against western international economic dominance, and perceived ideological and cultural hegemony by the 'west' over the 'rest'.

Key Asian values principles assert the primacy of community over individual rights, respect for family, authority, cooperation and social harmony over interest-based competition. Such values are claimed as a key cause for regional economic success. In institutional terms they support corporatist and state-capitalist rather than liberal pluralist models of political economy. However, Singapore's strict rule of law principles in commercial and criminal law, and meritocracy in the workplace, is nearer to the western outlook than patronage systems common elsewhere in Southeast Asia.

Asian values ideology reflects Singapore's 'core values', which have formed the basis for official ideology during the past two decades. Both tend to be legitimised in terms of Confucius' teachings. However, others have urged that Confucius nowhere advocates total individual subordination to state or community. Knowledge should be pursued for personal self-development as well as public service. Similar principles of personal growth pervade Hinduism and Buddhism, while individual responsibility and accountability are key principles within Islam.

A softer variant to the hard-line approach of the 'Singapore school' was initiated in a report prepared for the Commission for a New Asia by a diversity of Asian intellectuals brought together under the auspices of the Institute for Strategic and International Studies, Kuala Lumpur. The report offers a hybrid of communitarian and liberal perspectives. Asian countries are urged to be discriminating in absorbing external values, but to avoid blanket rejection and relativist extremes, which often serve to cover up internal deficiencies. Democratisation is affirmed, but with an emphasis on family values and social harmony, and 'constructive' as against litigious, interest group forms of politics and government. Distinctive features of Asian cultures, notably tolerance and appreciation for pluralism, should be preserved in the face of globalising trends.

Emphasis on the dignity of the human person is balanced by warnings that citizens possess both rights and duties. The idea that the state is everything and the individual nothing is rejected. But the individual cannot be placed above the community. Government 'of the people, by the people, for the people' requires guaranteed universal suffrage and public accountability of governments. Nevertheless, strong and responsible government is a virtue, not a vice. Stability is vital, but overcoming poverty equally so, to which end it is vital to root out corruption. The 'law of the jungle' in the form of unrestrained market economics is unacceptable and society must ensure that capitalism has a human face.

Notions of 'inter-civilisational dialogue' were promoted by a group close to former Malaysian Deputy Prime Minister Anwar Ibrahim. A leading role was played by Dr. Chandra Muzaffar, appointed as Director of the newly established Centre for Civilizational Dialogue at the University of Malaya in 1997. Non-renewal of Muzaffar's contract in April 1999 was widely seen as resulting from his outspoken support for Anwar Ibrahim following his downfall and imprisonment.

Ibrahim asserted that it is altogether shameful to cite Asian values as an excuse for autocratic practices and denial of basic rights and civil liberties. To say that freedom is Western or un-Asian is to offend our own traditions as well as our forefathers who gave their lives in the struggle against tyranny and injustice.

Regarding individual rights it is true that Asians lay great emphasis on order and societal stability. But it is certainly wrong to regard society as a kind of deity upon whose altar the individual must constantly be sacrificed. No Asian tradition can be cited to support the proposition that the individual must melt into a faceless community.

On the cultural front, Ibrahim urged that

> *for Asia to be truly global, its societies must be prepared to transform themselves and discard the harmful residue from the past tribalism, feudalism, narrow-mindedness and fanaticism Asia must not lose its identity, but it must renew commitment to core values such as justice, virtue and compassion, that are in themselves universal.*

Ibrahim further insisted on moral and intellectual equality. Former colonial rulers are urged to engage with Asians 'as equal partners in actualizing a new moral vision for the world.' Continued hectoring on human rights, conditionalities on trade and patronising cultural outlooks create suspicion of a hidden agenda, aimed at replacing old with new forms of domination.

Ibrahim's outlook is by no means secular or libertarian, as indicated by his emphasis on integrating religious and moral dimensions as a basis for strengthening community bonds. Rather he reflects the view of many Asian religious leaders and scholars that western hostility to religion derives from the secular rationalist and materialist values of the Enlightenment.

Inter-civilisational dialogue is not necessarily supportive of human rights. The idea arose partly in response to Huntington's clash of civilisations thesis, as did the original Asian values debate itself. Primary goals of tolerance, mutual understanding and peaceful resolution of disputes underlying the dialogue idea may result in new syncretisms which could undermine universal human rights. The idea's democratic intent is also uncertain. Mahbubani has expressed a conviction that the future lies in a fusion of civilisations, in a world in which the Asia-Pacific region will play a very substantial role. In that context, he argues that dialogue requires an intellectual 'level playing field' based on mutual respect for each others choices, and avoiding smug knee-jerk responses. For example, Singapore favours public safety and health relative to civil liberties of real and potential criminals compared with the USA. While legitimate arguments can be advanced on either side, each society must live with the consequences of its choices. Such principles have not discouraged Singapore from mocking at the Philippines' perceived combination of democratic politics and economic failure.

Some of the most telling criticism of Asian values has come from within Southeast Asia. Thus, Yash Ghai rejects claims by some government leaders to speak for the whole region in portraying universal human rights as western concepts without regional relevance. Other Asian voices, he asserts, whose culture has been destroyed by state imposed models of development, such as middle classes seeking more democracy, tribals and minorities, are now speaking out. Elites counter-attack, using developmentalist ideologies to justify domestic repression, while simultaneously demanding economic assistance from western countries, who may not question progress on civil and political rights.

Communitarian ideology supporting Asian values suffers from weaknesses of overstating the individualism of western societies and philosophies, and false equation of states with communities. Drastic state powers are employed to control and shape communities, and often to destroy them. Ghai claims that community organisation is more vital and lively in the 'individualist' west. Despite western countries' poor historical records, the concept of universal human rights contains potentially dynamic, transformative power in the Asian context, where people suffer major violations at the hands of both state and civil society.

The Asian Forum of NGOs held a parallel forum in Bangkok from 29 March to 2 April 1993 alongside the official UN regional consultation and issued their own alternative declaration of principles. These affirmed human rights as both universal and indivisible, according both major streams of rights full equality. Their statement provided the foundation for the Vienna Declaration and Programme of Action (VDPA) agreed two months later. The NGOs' position contrasts sharply with their governments, who formally accepted the VDPA but remained aloof from its action implications. The VDPA conflicts sharply with global neo-liberal outlooks, which are negative or indifferent to economic, social and cultural rights.

While there are many other dissenting non-state voices, such as students, intellectuals, journalists, trade unions and opposition political parties, NGOs appear most organisationally well adapted to networking, mobilisation, advocacy, information sharing and exploiting limited social space under restricted conditions. While the 'associational revolution' they are claimed to have effected may be overstated, their role in strengthening civil society and partially balancing state and business power is widely recognised. Diverse links with disadvantaged groups render most NGOs pluralist and inclusive in outlook, and therefore less inclined to see human rights advocacy as encroaching on national sovereignty. While Southeast Asian NGOs share common ground with their governments in attributing the poor state of human rights to an unjust international economic order, they link economic rights to a less statist view of development, more focused on equity and sustainability.

Some western commentary rejects Asian values discourse entirely, as based on selective interpretation of both western and Asian cultures, designed to legitimate power holders. Rodan and Hewison claim that Asian corporatist models of state and society reflect organic state theory originating in Europe. Neo-liberals and business interests are also attracted to East Asian states' capacity to discipline their work forces, thereby limiting welfare demands and related tax burdens characteristic of western social democracies. However, they find its interventionist and patrimonial aspects less acceptable. Robison argues that societal and structural change arising from East Asian industrialisation will soon necessitate sharp choices between introducing some form of welfare support or abandoning large masses to their market fate - anathema to Asian values-style communitarian rhetoric. Simultaneously, predatory and rent-seeking behaviour generate both local and international demands for rule of law and good governance which are hard to institutionalise outside a democratic framework.

Other scholars, both critical and supportive, accept the existence of Asian values as factually based. An example of the former is the illiberal democracy critique, whose contributors find both cultural substance and tools for state legitimation in Asian values claims. Conversely, Vatikiotis portrays Asian leaders as making skilful and pragmatic use of cultural tools in forging institutions appropriate to their countries' economic and social developmental needs. Others calling for dialogue accept that Asian values polemic reflects genuine cultural concerns.

Asianist scholars increasingly cooperate in comparative studies, seeking to avoid imposing external interpretations on societies with very different histories, institutions, economy and ecology, yet recognising wide diversity across the region.

Democracy and Asian Values

Notions of 'Asian democracy' are interwoven with Asian values discourse. While the details of proposed models differ between countries, common features include Confucian-style values, patron-client relations, personalised authority, dominant political party, and strong state. It is unclear whether Asian variants are intended to permanently replace western-style liberal democracy, or provide a transition towards it. Though almost universally accepted as the currency of political legitimacy, 'democracy' has never been tied down, as in the west, to particular institutions and processes, and operates within an environment of free-floating meanings and associations.

Asian values protagonists claim that their concerns centre on contextualised application rather than principle. But they urge emphasis on good governance and performance over process, and decry western countries' unwillingness to accept responsibility for instability when imperfect governments are overthrown as a result of pressures for democratisation and human rights.

In ideal-type terms, Asian democracy paradigms propose an antithesis between values of state, authority, national unity, community, stability, development and harmony as against individualism, egoism, hedonism, legalism and anarchy. This can be restated from a liberal-democratic perspective in terms of conflict between liberty, pluralism, rule of law, equality, accountability and participation against autocracy, repression, militarism, corruption and exploitation.

In practice, Asian political systems mix many combinations of democratic and non-democratic elements. New terms such as 'illiberal' and 'semi' democracy attempt to grapple with this reality. Such hybrids are proving more resilient than paradigms which either polarise opposites or predict a natural evolution towards liberal democracy in line with an 'end of history' thesis.

Both western and Asian democracies confront the reality of plural societies with competing moral, social, and political outlooks. Accommodating minorities poses a challenge to principles of democratic majoritarianism in both. While liberal-democracies tend to favour constitutional or legislative safeguards for minority rights, East Asian states tend to manipulate their societies' diversity to impose their own models of harmony and national integration.

In terms of mechanisms, liberal-democrats place their faith, based on scepticism towards fallible rulers, in separation of powers, rules and processes, checks and balances. By contrast, there is strong East Asian cultural resistance to such notions, reflecting the Chinese proverb that there is 'only one sun in the sky'. Cultural preference for concentrating authority similarly de-legitimises boundaries between state and civil society and supports integralist and corporatist political systems. Federalism and other kinds of regional and local devolution of powers are similarly suspect, as are notions of 'rule of law' which limit political leaders' operational discretion. Consequently, while preserving democratic forms, political elites devise means to control or limit the powers and composition of parliaments, and ensure that ruling parties or coalitions remain dominant.

Asian democracy practitioners deny that political opposition is necessarily beneficial, stressing potential divisions and factionalism. Consequently, much dissent takes the form of proposing alternative solutions within the framework of official ideology and institutions. A multi-party structure may be tolerated, as in Malaysia, as a means of articulating communal interests within a pluralist society, without threatening dominant power structures. For liberals, genuine electoral competition and the real prospect of opposition parties gaining government represents a basic test of whether a system is democratic.

Malaysia's system has now been established in much its present form for three decades, reflecting entrenched features of its society and politics. However, there can be no certainty whether it will shift over time in a democratic or authoritarian direction. Despite gradual consolidation of democratic rule, the convolutions of the Thai situation were captured in Donald Emmerson's description of its regime as a 'military-influenced multi-party parliamentary-democratic constitutional monarchy'. The case for regarding the Philippines as less than fully democratic, despite extensive constitutional and other reforms since 1986, rests on the continuing dominance of oligarchic elites over processes of law and politics in the regions, criminalisation and corruption in public life and disregard for human rights in many areas.

Notions of transition imply ultimate adoption of a western liberal model. Realistically, many combinations of democratic and authoritarian rule are possible. Ironically, the two countries which started out with Westminster-style democracy, Singapore and Malaysia, are in a stronger position to maintain ruling party dominance than those which have moved to democratic rule after a long period of military dominance, such as Thailand and Indonesia. Singapore's government, from a seemingly impregnable position, is seeking ways of mobilising greater participation for purposes of problem-solving, yet without adopting liberal democratic processes.

Writing before the Asian economic crisis, Jayasuriya saw democratic transition as based on re-negotiation of intra-state relations, driven by changing needs of capitalist development. Although such re-negotiation may include new elements of the emerging middle class and previously excluded fractions of capital, Jayasuriya insists that the wider civil society will be excluded. This view discounts massive popular upheavals in Indonesia, and earlier mobilisation which contributed to overthrowing authoritarian rule in the Philippines in 1986 and Thailand in 1992.

Earlier optimism that the 'middle class' would represent a driving force for democratic change has become more qualified. Many professionals and business groups depend on their governments for survival. They also fear potential disorder and multiplication of demands from mass democratic empowerment. David Jones considers that many planners and administrators have internalised Confucian-style values of obedience and conformity in an anxious search for certainty and continuity in fast changing times. Nevertheless, middle and lower-middle class elements with some level of educational achievement frequently assist popular mobilisation among workers, peasants and other disadvantaged groups.

Both advocates and critics of Asian democracy approaches agree on the pivotal roles played by states in shaping economic development and political culture and processes. This picture is confirmed, irrespective of constitutional forms, when individual ASEAN countries are compared in subsequent sections.

Democracy and Development in Southeast Asia

Most ASEAN governments rated development more highly than human rights and democracy goals in the early 1990s. They showed correspondingly little awareness of contradictions entailed in demanding equality between different streams of rights, while insisting on development as a pre-condition for civil and political rights. At the 1993 UN regional consultation, only the Philippines refused to accept that economic development must entail sacrifice of individual and political rights, asserting that the nation's recent experience had demonstrated that this was a false choice.

Outdoing Huntington and even Marx, Mahbubani sees economic development as probably the most subversive force in history in promoting political and social change. 'By comparison, the Aquino revolution in the Philippines and award of the Nobel Peace Prize to Aung San Suu Kyi are mere symbols, which barely make a dent in the lives of the teeming billions suffering poverty in developing countries.' As yet, however, Singapore's outstanding economic success has not resulted in political liberalisation.

Attempts to link economic aid with human rights performance are sternly rebuked. Donor criteria should focus on promoting good government, applying key tests of political stability, sound administration, meritocracy, economic growth with equity, fiscal prudence and relative lack of corruption. Change occurs slowly, in most cases requiring cooperation with existing governments. Only states which have allowed their people to stagnate for decades, such as Myanmar and North Korea, deserve condemnation.

The relative weakness of the domestic private sector at independence, especially among indigenous groups, has required governments to play leading roles in late industrialising, post-colonial Southeast Asia. Complex networks have subsequently developed between governments, foreign and domestic capital, with favoured groups developing a local capitalist base, although often of the rent-seeking rather than entrepreneurial kind. While abrupt withdrawal of the state from economic involvement could prove destructive, transparent, efficient and equitable management of scarce resources is essential to fulfilling basic economic and social rights on a mass scale.

Popular expectations of governments are ambivalent. A traditional Burmese prayer asking deliverance from fire, famine, disease, flood and government can be set alongside popular quests for a just ruler. While common experience of corruption and exploitation drives the prayer, the mark of the just ruler is to provide security, discipline corrupt officials and ensure peoples' subsistence. This latter is seen as a primary task of economic development. But Southeast Asians, while less concerned about censorship of interference in their personal lives, tend to see welfare as the responsibility of families or religious charity. With the exception of Singapore, they appear less interested in health and safety issues, over which western governments are expected to exercise stringent controls.

The role of the state in development and the appropriateness of democratic relative to authoritarian systems of government in its achievement are closely interlinked issues. Unfortunately they have been conflated to produce a falsely polarised choice between a democratic state progressively withdrawing itself from economic involvement and an interventionist state based on authoritarian rule.

One side argues that liberal-style democracy, as a key element in good governance, brings virtues of accountability, transparency and legal regularisation essential to economic management and planning. Personal freedom is claimed as encouraging entrepreneurship, thereby enhancing wealth and prosperity, widening education, skills and sense of competence. Democratic processes build capacity for negotiation and compromise, as the basis of good citizenship. Exposure to western ideas as part of globalisation provides further reinforcement.

Counter-arguments depict sterile competition between groups unable to perceive wider national interests and objectives, as paralysing or seriously slowing down national development. Electoral competition requires their appeasement by means of short term fixes and benefits. Only strong governments are capable of taking difficult, often unpopular decisions necessary to bring longer term benefits. An inversion of this argument is that high rates of growth widen the wealth gap, necessitating authoritarian rule in order to suppress discontent. Both Prime Minister Mahathir of Malaysia and former Philippines President Ferdinand Marcos have argued for democratic freedoms to be rationed out sparingly, for fear of hampering economic growth.

Lee Kuan Yew, in one of his periodic forays into Filipino politics, commented that development requires discipline. This can be undermined by too 'exuberant' forms of democracy, resulting in corruption and stagnation, particularly where 'gridlock' of the American variety occurs. President Ramos responded that democracy is intrinsic to development and warned against throwing away hard won political gains for a 'quick fix'. Some Filipinos, reported as agreeing with Lee, see American emphasis on individualism as undermining Filipino community values.

Human rights-based concepts of development emphasise basic physical wellbeing, human dignity and opportunities for self-development, with rights to participate in shaping relevant public policy and institutions. The Human Development Index (HDI), devised by the United Nations Development Programme (UNDP), provides a general measure of welfare, combining life expectancy at birth; education based on adult literacy and mean years of schooling and income. UNDP's annual Human Development Reports are developing a progressively more comprehensive picture, supplementing HDI with disaggregated data relating to regions, ethnic, gender and other socio-economic groups, linked to macro and micro income and expenditure data.

HDI ranking gives no clear correlation with democratic orientation. Neher and Marlay categorised Southeast Asian countries as democratic, semi-democratic, semi-authoritarian and authoritarian on the basis of citizen participation, electoral competition and civil liberties. The Philippines, Thailand and Malaysia were classed, in descending order, as semi-democratic; Singapore and Indonesia as semi-authoritarian. The four poorest states - Myanmar, Laos, Cambodia and Vietnam - plus the richest in per capita terms, Brunei, are categorised as authoritarian. Brunei's HDI ranks second among ASEAN states, only slightly below Singapore. Their successes in delivering economic and social human rights offer *prima facie* support for Asian democracy claims favouring strong government, although their special features as city-state and oil rich kingdom with relatively small populations must be taken into account.

The Philippines experienced economic decline under both Marcos and his immediate democratic successor. Judgements that most Filipinos were too preoccupied with subsistence, preventing them from participating in the political life of the nation raise issues of comparison - for example, with the USA where deep pockets of poverty still exist and where electoral turnout even for Presidential elections barely exceeds 50 per cent. Malaysia, the most authoritarian of the three countries classified as 'semi-democratic', ranks third in terms of both GDP and HDI indicators. But the deeply authoritarian nature of the lowest income ASEAN countries can be seen as negatively reinforcing pro-democracy arguments.

Table 2.1. ASEAN Human Development Index and Gross Domestic Product ($ US) 1997

	Real GDP per capita	**HDI value**	**HDI ranking**
Singapore	28,460	0.888	22
Brunei	29,773	0.878	25
Malaysia	8,140	0.768	56
Thailand	6,690	0.753	67
Philippines	3,520	0.740	77
Indonesia	3,490	0.681	105
Vietnam	1,630	0.664	110
Myanmar	1,199	0.580	128
Cambodia	1,290	0.514	137
Laos	1,300	0.491	140

World Bank analysis currently posits strong links between democratic participation and economic growth. Changes in mental outlook central to development, it is argued, will not reach deep into the society if changes are introduced without open and extensive discussion. Inclusive processes are more likely to generate a wider sense of ownership towards new policies and practices. External imposition of 'best practice' by means of conditionalities or other pressures may fail to produce lasting change, undermining incentives to develop peoples' own capacities. For these reasons, often 'maddeningly slow' processes of democracy may yield more sustainable results than authoritarian quick fixes. Also, the knowledge and communications revolution is transforming economic and production structures in ways which require cooperative modes of problem-solving rather than vertical industrial structures employed in coordinating masses of workers for purposes of assembly line production.

The economic costs of weak financial regulatory frameworks, linked to lack of transparency and accountability, became starkly apparent during the recent regional crisis. A democratically empowered citizenry, it is claimed, would have demanded swifter and stronger action against fraud and mismanagement, while threats of civil action will in future provide a sharper spur to legal enforcement. Weak governance discourages investment, and dissipates the effectiveness of aid programs. Asian democracy advocates claim that their models are designed with precisely these problems in view. Liberals retort that if individuals have a voice in shaping changes, they are more likely to be internalised and accepted over the longer term.

Regional Economic Crisis

The economic crisis, beginning in mid-1997, and its aftermath have posed fundamental threats to the economic and social rights of Southeast Asians. However, the experience has brought issues of democracy and human rights to the fore, revitalising debates over economic development strategy. While there was evidence of recovery by mid-1999, the original causes of the crisis remain in dispute.

All East Asian countries were seriously affected, with Indonesia, Thailand and South Korea suffering the worst effects. For around three decades, GDP per capita had grown by at least five per cent annually in these countries and Malaysia, with still higher average growth rates in Singapore. Growth had brought increased educational opportunity and dramatic reduction in poverty rates. Indonesian poverty declined from 64 per cent in 1975 to 11 per cent in 1995. Secondary school enrolment rates doubled in East Asia over twenty-five years. The countries cited above saved over one-third of their GDP prior to the crisis, compared with the US national savings rate of 17 per cent.

Currency devaluations, beginning with the Thai baht, were most severe in the case of the Indonesian rupiah, which fell from 2,500 to 17,000 to the US dollar at one stage, fluctuating throughout 1998 between 7,500 and 15,000. Devaluation, as both cause and consequence of rising indebtedness, resulted in an abrupt credit squeeze and rising interest rates, with a chain reaction of business closures and worker layoffs. The World Bank warned of fifty million people returning to poverty in Indonesia, with twenty million set to lose their jobs. 1.5 million were laid off in South Korea, while unemployment rose from 1.8 at the end of 1997 to 2.7 million jobless in Thailand six months later. Governments compensated for revenue losses with severe cuts in health, education, other public and social services. Prices for fuel, food and other necessities rose sharply. Longer term damage will have been caused by loss of schooling and malnutrition suffered by millions of children.

According to the World Bank, household strategies to cope with falling family incomes included cutting back on food spending, thus increasing vulnerability to illness;

withdrawing children from school to supplement household income or undertake household chores; cutting back on medical expenditures. Women suffered worst, losing their jobs first and providing for their families before themselves. Violence against women also increased as a result of heightened social conflict.

There was significant social unrest among workers laid off in Thailand and South Korea. However, apart from Indonesia where protest extended more widely as part of a more general political crisis, violence was substantially contained. In Malaysia, public protest was very moderate, and did not become violent until the dismissal and arrest of Deputy Prime Minister, Ibrahim. While the crisis helped influence popular sentiment in favour of change, major focus was on daily survival. Policy debate was similarly reactive.

Asian values polemic became muted, and a source of some embarrassment in the light of the crisis, generating a quiet sense of relief, even complacency among westerners that the subject could now be quietly dropped. Much neo-liberal commentary has been triumphalist, pointing out the dire consequences of intervention and cronyism by authoritarian governments as evidence of the illusory, or at least contingent nature of Asian values, with virtues now seemingly turned into vices.

Such attitudes have fuelled resentment among some Asian leaders. Dr. Mahathir, bitterly attacked the destructive behaviour of international currency speculators. Far from being merely an expression of market forces, the crisis had been deliberately engineered, he alleged, by forces in the west alarmed by Asian economic success and determined to defeat challenges to their domination. If Asian countries were forced to submit to globalisation on western terms, with westerners using the opportunity to buy up local companies at bargain prices, resentment would persist, possibly leading to some form of revenge via guerilla warfare.

Most attempts at explanation begin with a long list of perceived problems, leading to the assumption that any problem that existed prior to the crisis is automatically part of its cause. Thus the supposedly special Asian mixture of government intervention and market capitalism was widely acclaimed as contributing strongly to the supposed economic miracle. Yet an excess of one or both was freely blamed for the subsequent crisis. Authoritarianism was also identified as a prime cause. Yet Singapore, adapting earlier prescriptions, weathered the storm better than all others in East Asia. Recently democratising South Korea and Thailand, which had been regarded as model pupils of International Monetary Fund (IMF) neo-liberal orthodoxy, were the worst sufferers after Indonesia, while the region's most closed economies, the socialist countries and Myanmar, remained relatively untouched, albeit at very low levels of development.

Fierce controversy has surrounded the role of the IMF, seen by its detractors as more cause than cure of East Asia's economic woes. Its standard prescriptions call for balanced budgets, credit restrictions and higher interest rates, liberalisation of the financial sector, public spending cuts, dismantling of price controls, import barriers and restrictions on capital movements, and privatisation of public enterprises. However, in East Asia the problem was one of private sector debt rather than budgetary imbalance. Removal of subsidies on fuel and food in May 1998 provided an immediate trigger for riots in Indonesia. Delays in disbursement of IMF funds, due to resistance to its terms by recipient governments and conditionalities imposed by the US Congress, further aggravated the crisis.

Criticism of the IMF has been by no means confined to radical ideologues or Asian nationalists. World Bank President, James Wolfensohn, complained that emphasis on billion dollar rescue packages was obscuring the crisis' human and social dimensions. To place such differences in context, the World Bank's focus is more broadly developmental, while the IMF's brief mainly covers currency and financial management. IMF 'structural adjustment' programmes nevertheless entail deep incursions into countries' macro economic policy-making. During the 1980s, the World Bank had adopted a broadly neo-liberal outlook supporting privatisation, de-regulation and export-oriented industrialisation. This contrasted with its earlier, Keynesian-style mixed economy approach, influenced by redistribution-with-growth and 'basic needs' strategies. By the early 1990s, revived concerns over poverty and social impact, brought renewed emphasis on equity, and some re-casting of neo-liberal policies in terms of 'adjustment with a human face'.

A comprehensive effort to address the crisis was mounted at a regional meeting in Bangkok on 21-22 January 1999, initiated jointly by the IMF and the World Bank. Two hundred and thirty delegates, representing ninety-six countries, donor, and civil society delegations concluded that official policy and rhetoric of decentralisation and empowerment was not matched by adequate listening required to accurately gauge the needs, objectives and capacities of poor families and communities. There was also an incomplete understanding of social and family breakdown among the poor. Governments should adopt facilitating and cooperative rather than command roles, in turn requiring major changes in political culture among politicians and administrators, unwilling to devolve either resources or authority. This also implies changes in people's expectations of governments - seen in most societies as providers, enforcers and problem-solvers of both first and last resort.

Within this general framework, the World Bank announced plans to nearly triple its new lending commitments to social sectors over a three-year period, including $6 billion channelled directly to governments through Structural Adjustment Loans (SALs). The Korean $2 billion loans contained guidelines for labour market reforms and strengthening social safety nets. The Indonesian $1 billion SAL focused on maintaining availability of key goods with only modest price increases, initiatives to maintain access to quality basic education and health, and labour-intensive public works programmes.

The UNDP continued to promote balancing human with economic development, if need be accepting lower growth rates in the interests of equity. Policies designed to minimise disproportionately negative impact on the poor and maximise opportunities for them from globalisation included managing trade and capital flows more carefully, investing in poor people, particularly among farmers and the informal sector, stimulating exports from small enterprises, managing new technology, setting safety nets for the poor, and improving governance. While the financial cost of such policies was proportionately modest, the political will and administrative skills required are considerable. Their effectiveness also depends considerably on empowerment of relevant communities.

The UNDP's mandate requires it to deal officially only with governments, preventing it from confronting IMF policies directly, although oblique criticism was indicated by Phillips Young, Resident Representative of UNDP in Malaysia, Singapore and Brunei, who warned of the management and social consequences arising from too rapid growth, and urged that financial recovery measures that exacerbate emerging social problems should be 'avoided like the plague'.

Can a workable consensus for change emerge from such debates, or will a 'dialogue of the deaf' ensure continuation of 'business as usual'? Ideological polarisation persists between Asian and neo-liberal cum globalising versions of democracy and governance. Both detract from any systematic focus on universal human rights, all forms of which have been damaged by the economic crisis, despite important democratic openings. The East versus West polemic flowing from both streams of discourse is similarly unhelpful to developing cooperation necessary to addressing both global and local dimensions of the crisis and its aftermath.

Singapore

Singapore achieved independence initially as part of Malaysia in 1963, from which it separated in 1965. As a small island state, imperatives of survival have always dominated Singapore's strategic outlook, with strong emphasis on social discipline, political authority and stability as the foundation for economic prosperity. Maintaining harmony between the three major ethnic and religious groups is a fundamental priority. Economic development has been impressive in both growth and distributional terms, with real GDP surpassing that of most western countries. Excellent standards of health, housing and education have been achieved for the vast majority of Singaporeans, funded by compulsory payments to the Central Provident Fund (CPF).

Singapore's political system has remained firmly under civilian control from the outset, with regular elections every five years. The People's Action Party (PAP) has dominated the political scene since it swept to power in 1959. Long-serving Prime Minister, Lee Kuan Yew stepped down in 1991, but retains strong influence as Senior Minister. International observers accept the electoral process itself as honestly conducted, though some Singaporeans are uncertain as to the secrecy of the ballot, in a context of pervasive government scrutiny of citizens.

The PAP held all Parliamentary seats from 1965 until 1981, when the Workers' Party candidate S. Jeyaratnam won a by-election. Opposition parties gained ground very slowly thereafter, winning only four out of eighty-one seats by 1992, reduced to two in 1997. While opposition parties regularly receive between 30 and 40 per cent of the popular vote, this is fragmented in a 'first past the post' electoral system. Gaining representation was made more difficult for poorly resourced parties by the introduction of enlarged multi-member electorates. This change has also strengthened minority ethnic representation among PAP parliamentarians. Provision has been made for a few candidates who come closest to gaining election to serve as Nominated Members of Parliament, though with reduced powers.

During the 1960s and 1970s, opposition centred on the Barisan Socialist party, labelled left-wing by the PAP and reflecting earlier socio-cultural divisions between English and Chinese educated among the majority community. These became less relevant following elimination of non-English medium schools. During the 1980s and 1990s, the opposition flag was carried by the Workers' Party and Singapore Democratic party. Both proposed very moderate reform platforms, which assumed their continuance in opposition. Recognising continuing popular support for the PAP and its entrenched powers, appeals to voters were couched in terms of electing a few opposition members in order to provide some balance and critical voice. In 1992 and 1997, nominations were put forward for less than half the electorates, thus ensuring a PAP victory before polling day.

Despite such efforts at reassurance, notions of opposition as necessarily beneficial have been attacked as contrary to Singaporean notions of good government. After the 1997 election, Prime Minister Goh Chock Tong labelled 'opposition for its own sake' as an unwanted feature of western liberal democracy, and called on opposition parties to propose comprehensive alternative programmes. In principle, this would legitimise genuine electoral competition, which the government has never explicitly opposed. However, alternatives are hard to develop, given the PAP's proclivity to take out libel suits against criticism deemed unfair or inaccurate. The more fundamental problem lies with opposition parties' lack of ideological, policy and organisational coherence. Consequently, opposition has mostly been articulated by a series of courageous individuals, notably S. Jeyaratnam, Francis Seow and Chee Soon Juan.

Civil and political rights in Singapore's outwardly Westminster-style political system are constrained by a range of powerful legal and structural obstacles. These include sweeping internal security legislation, controls over media, rights to organise and public protest. Student activity on campus is tightly regulated, while labour relations are controlled within a tripartite framework comprising union, employer and government representatives. High wages and benefits, such as fair price shops and recreation facilities in return for constantly improved productivity have helped to make such arrangements acceptable to workers. Foreign publications selling over 300 copies locally must be licensed and funds deposited against any legal suits. If declared to be engaging in domestic politics, they can be banned or their sales restricted. However, such restrictions are increasingly by-passed via cyberspace information channels, despite efforts to introduce controls in these areas also.

Scope for growth of autonomous social movements or any but strictly recreational, cultural or welfare-oriented associations is similarly circumscribed. Religious bodies are constrained from involvement in public issues by laws which forbid any mingling of religion and politics. State assumption of a right to define the nature of religion implied here sets limits to freedom of religion itself. State domination over civil society has been enhanced by establishment of residents' associations, through which all policy suggestions and requests for services must be directed. While genuine community leaders can play active consultative roles, Members of Parliament, who chair such bodies, act as the only effective channel for representing local needs at higher levels. Since 1988, MPs also head town councils. Local councils are responsible for administering housing estates, giving them significant control over the lives of residents in public housing, which accommodates around 80 per cent of the population, including an increasing proportion of private owners. Disadvantages of electing an opposition representative in this situation are obvious.

Asian values paradigms underlie Singapore's own core values, declared in 1989. These include familiar principles of community over self, upholding the family as the basic building-block of society, consensus rather than conflict and maintaining racial and religious harmony. Community support for the individual was added by Goh Chock Tong, soon after his appointment as Prime Minister, to harsher earlier formulations stressing subordination of individuals to authority. Goh also called for the building of a nation of character and grace based on dignity and mutual support.

Vasil argues that re-emphasis on Chinese culture, including the campaign to learn the Mandarin language, was aimed both at consolidating the Chinese community and as a corrective to earlier policies which had constrained its expression in order to reassure ethnic minorities. Indian and Malay sense of disadvantage has been partially addressed via special training and enterprise promotion bodies, designed to equalise opportunities without infringing principles of meritocracy zealously pursued by the government. But expressions of ethnic and religious identity which might emphasise difference from other groups or identify with overseas conflicts are strictly excluded.

Partial re-construction of Singapore identity around consolidation of ethnoreligious communities has created uncertainty regarding principles of secularism. Emphasis on family authority holds potentially negative consequences for women by reinforcing patriarchy, while devolution of authority to community leaders constrains freedom of religious and cultural choice. Partly in order to shore up the Malay vote and maintain social harmony, and partly out of concern to avoid conflict with powerful neighbours, religious conversions and inter-religious marriages, particularly in cases involving Moslems, are quietly discouraged.

Support for the PAP is likely to continue at a high level, given its capacity to maintain prosperity amidst surrounding instability, with most Singaporeans accepting government arguments that strong political authority, social order, economic and technological progress are closely integrated. Initiative for change may ultimately emerge from within the state system itself, with some government leaders recognising an underlying problem of participation. Rapid change linked to globalisation require cooperative problem-solving at many social levels. Passivity and conformity in the political sphere by an increasingly well-educated population can only be maintained by ever more convoluted forms of managerialism.

Prospects for opening up new participatory channels within existing corporatist frameworks, as alternatives to western-style political liberalisation, were signalled by Deputy Prime Minister, Lee Hsien Loong, who has urged the need to coopt people and ideas at all levels and to adopt more open approaches to governance and administration. Apparently qualifying earlier doctrines about the need for strong authority, Lee observed that outside observers, perhaps not understanding how consensus building works in Singapore, sometimes attribute our ability to make fast and drastic changes to our lack of freedom and dictatorial methods. If coercion and regimentation were the secrets of success, the highest growth rate in Asia would be North Korea.

Active citizenship must, therefore, move beyond consultation to partnership in both private and public sectors, which will in turn require a major reorientation of outlook within the civil service.

Lee Hsien Loong's concept will presumably also require re-evaluation of Confucian notions of governance by wise leaders. These are likely to be retained in some form in order to focus on problem-solving rather than encourage populist demands. Rule of law, which operates impeccably in the criminal, civil and business spheres, will remain limited by executive discretion in areas deemed too sensitive for public debate - though criteria for identifying 'out of bounds' markers is itself emerging as a subject of public discourse. Effective participatory processes cannot be developed without clearly defined rights, linked to regularised systems of law and representation. Contradictions here are reflected in the replacement of executive intervention via internal security provisions by more legalistic resort to libel actions and tax audits against opposition figures. Artificial separation between political, civil and commercial spheres will become increasingly difficult in the face of increasing market liberalisation, wider consumer choices and information flows.

Singapore's experience has so far refuted the idea that liberal democracy must automatically flow from economic prosperity. Its corporatist structures have proved resilient, retaining a high measure of popular legitimacy. Political opponents have proved unable to aggregate issues, let alone offer coherent alternatives. Pervasive state penetration of civil society, plus a cautious and materialist outlook among the middle class, discourages open debate necessary to building a democratic culture. Yet it would be surprising if increasingly high levels of excellence achieved in the economic, technological and scientific spheres did not ultimately result in calls for wider political participation.

The Philippines

The Philippines gradually faded from the international human rights spotlight following the overthrow of President Marcos in April 1986. During Marcos' fourteen year rule, basic civil and political rights were suspended, and detentions without trial, torture and 'salvaging' of labour, peasant, women, students and social activists by military, para-military, thugs and vigilantes became rife. Marcos was eventually forced to step down by a coalition between a broad-based 'people's power' movement and a military reform faction, with some assistance from the USA. These events followed a Presidential election contest between Marcos and Mrs. Corazaon Aquino. Monitoring by the National Movement for Free Elections (NAMFREL) and international observers revealed widespread ballot fraud, confirmed by a walkout of electoral officials.

With expiry of his second Presidential term imminent, Marcos' justified seizing power in 1972 on grounds of instability from communist and other insurgencies, corruption and the need to focus on economic development. Politics was recast around the government-controlled New Society Movement (KBL), structured along similar lines to Indonesia's Golkar organisation. Marcos' position was legitimised by constitutional changes which replaced the Philippines' US-style Presidential system with one reflecting that prevailing in France, where a Prime Minister and Cabinet are responsible to Parliament but the President retains substantial executive powers to overrule and dismiss Parliament. Marcos held both top positions until 1984 under various interim arrangements.

During the early years of martial law, Marcos' attacks on patronage, corruption, money politics and violence (popularly known as 'guns, goons and gold'), prevalent in pre-1972 politics struck a popular chord, as did his emphasis on economic development. Early opposition focused on concentrations of power and wealth associated with dominant development models. Protests focused on land and labour issues, particularly exploitation of women in export processing zones. Mass-based social movements emerged, which generated demands for political change. The Catholic Church, despite its historical conservatism, lent significant support at many levels. The murder of Marcos' main political opponent, Senator 'Ninoy' Aquino, in 1983 galvanised the middle class into demanding a return to constitutional democracy.

There was nevertheless widespread scepticism about returning to narrowly-based intra-elite conflict characterising pre-1972 electoral politics, if this entailed leaving structural imbalances in power and wealth untouched. Divisions sharpened between those whose first priority was restoring electoral democracy and basic civil and political rights, and groups seeking more basic social and economic transformation linked to broader understandings of democratic participation. Calls for boycott of the 1986 Presidential elections by leftist coalitions were ignored by most voters, but similar ideological and tactical differences persisted into the post-Marcos era. Ultimately a measure of convergence has been achieved. While restoration of an essentially liberal democratic system reflected long established Philippines' political culture, mobilisation of civil society against Marcos substantially broadened political awareness, organising capacity and participation to include a wide range of new groups and agendas.

Following President Corazaon Aquino's accession, a new constitution was approved by popular referendum in February 1987. This restored the main features of the US-style 1935 constitution, but with important variations. These include a Bill of Rights, covering freedom of speech, assembly, access to bail and legal assistance, public information and official documents, freedom from detention without due process of law, torture, loss of property without compensation and prohibition of religious tests for public office. Extensive provisions in Article XIII for 'Social Justice and human rights' cover social and economic rights across all major groups and sectors. Article XII on 'National Economy and Patrimony' requires an active state role in promoting economic development and use of resources for national benefit. Sections 17-19 of Article XIII provide for institution of a national Commission on Human Rights.

In an effort to limit concentrations of power, the President is limited to one six-year term. The Chair of both the Civil Service and Electoral Commissions may serve only one term, and may not have contested immediately preceding elections. Key public officers may be removed by impeachment initiated by the House of Representatives, to be tried by the Senate. House members may serve a maximum of three three-year terms and senators two six-year terms. The independence of the Supreme Court was entrenched, together with full rights of judicial review.

In order to broaden representation in the 250 member House of Representatives, 80 per cent are elected on a proportional representation cum electoral district basis, with 20 per cent appointed from party lists on a nation-wide basis. As well as giving smaller parties some representation, it was provided that for three terms after ratification, half the party list seats would be allocated to labour, peasant, urban poor, cultural minorities, women, youth and other sectors provided by law. Congress was instructed to provide for referendums to be initiated by 10 per cent of voters, with at least 3 per cent from each legislative district. Requirements for autonomy of provincial and local government, linked to democratic reforms and allocation of revenues on an automatic basis, were substantially implemented via the 1991 Local Government Code, which also requires the transfer of many national officials to local government service.

The transition from military to civilian rule under President Aquino was disturbed by several coup attempts. These were defeated through the loyalty and vigilance of Defence Secretary General Fidel Ramos, who had held a top military position under Marcos, but had led the Reform of the Armed Forces Movement (RAM) together with Juan Ponce Enrile, who later turned against Aquino's administration. Her dependence on Ramos for political survival necessitated giving the military considerable freedom of action in combating the still active New People's Army (NPA) and Moslem secession movements in Mindanao. Such powers were often used indiscriminately against labour, peasant and other cause-oriented groups, with 'low intensity' counter-insurgency strategies promoting campaigns of propaganda and disinformation against both local and overseas supporters. These used local vigilante groups operating as a form of civil guard, trained and equipped by the military but largely beyond legal controls.

Reports of human rights abuses, and killings of activists consequently equalled or even exceeded those of the Marcos period, with investigations of earlier crimes scaled down.

President Ramos, elected in 1992 from a field of seven candidates with a primary vote of slightly under 25 per cent, was able to construct a workable coalition, enabling him to focus major attention on economic development. Annual growth had averaged 0.9 per cent between 1980 and 1992, with real per capita income down by 7.2 per cent over the same period. Thus, the Philippines' performance did not match that of other ASEAN neighbours who, prior to the 1997 currency crisis, could credibly claim a link between authoritarian rule and high economic growth rates. Economic stagnation during Marcos' rule and the transitional period under Aquino was widely attributed to dominance of monopolies and cartels linked to state-based patronage networks. Ramos promoted policies of liberalisation and privatised infrastructure development. Annual growth rates reached 6.8 per cent in 1996. World Bank assistance to continue structural reform and anti-poverty programmes in the face of the regional economic crisis was stepped up with a loan of US $3 billion in December 1997 and approximately US $4.5 billion pledged in March 1999.

The Ramos administration introduced a Social Reform Agenda programme. Its 'Minimum Needs' approach embracing thirty-three indicators and targeting twenty poorest provinces, supposedly identified after extensive national consultations. But only marginal reduction of chronically unequal income distribution was achieved, with the share of the lowest 20 per cent of the population rising from 5 to 5.9 per cent from 1970-75 to 1990-96. During the same period the share of the highest 20 per cent declined from 56 to 49.6 per cent. The Marcos administration did not record poverty data, but official poverty incidence declined between 1985 and 1994 from 49.2 to 40.2 per cent based on income measurement and from 32.7 to 23.4 per cent on expenditure measurement. Average annual population growth rate declined only gradually between 1970-75 and 1990-96 from 2.8 to 2.3 per cent, with opposition from the Catholic Church inhibiting the impact of official programmes.

Encouraged by the restoration of democracy, the presence of NGOs and other advocacy groups post-Marcos became pervasive across all fields of policy and social action. Competition for influence became intense, not least with political parties who commonly see themselves as prime agents for popular representation, and may resent potential challenges to their capacity to dispense patronage and protection. Both Presidents Aquino and Ramos made strong efforts to involve NGOs in decision-making processes, institutionalising their role within the Local Government Code. Assessments of their performance in terms of capacity, outlook and autonomy from the state and other powerful interests has varied widely.

President Estrada was elected in 1998 with strong support from poorer groups. Rapprochement with Marcos family and associates, and proposals for constitutional change which would allow Presidents a second term soon built up strong opposition among both the urban middle class and social activist groups. Confidence in the autonomy of Filipino media was called into question by Estrada's threats of libel action against the *Manila Times*, causing it to apologise unreservedly for allegations of corruption against presidential palace staff. The apology caused divisions among senior staff, evoking a strong statement by journalists, intellectuals and others claiming that the affair undermined press freedom.

By 2000, accusations of gross corruption and misappropriation of funds led to calls for Estrada's impeachment from Catholic Church leaders, business groups and a broad spectrum of popular advocacy groups. Under procedures laid down in Article XI, Section 3 of the Constitution, one-third of the House of Representatives may vote for impeachment, which requires a two-thirds majority in the Senate to succeed. In that event, the Vice-President assumes the President's powers.

Motions for impeachment on charges of 'economic plunder', which carry the death penalty under Filipino law, passed the House of Representatives on 13 September 2000. As the President sought the necessary eight Senators to reject the charges, Vice-President Arroyo was threatened with sedition charges by Estrada supporters for calling for the President's resignation. Expectations of acquittal were confirmed on 16 January 2001, when the Senate, by an 11-10 majority, rejected calls to compel disclosure of crucial information concerning bank accounts. Prosecutors walked out, compelling Presiding Officer Chief Justice Hilario Davide to adjourn proceedings pending action by the House of Representatives. Popular anger spilled on to the streets, with several violent clashes between pro and anti-Estrada demonstrators. On 19 January, Estrada left the Presidential Palace and was declared as unable to govern. Arroyo was sworn in as President. Estrada asserted his continuing status as President. The Supreme Court subsequently ruled against him, clearing the way for criminal and fraud charges.

Serious questions continue to be raised over the constitutionality of Estrada's ouster by commentators as diverse as Lee Kuan Yew and leftist veterans from the 'people's power' movement which overthrew Ferdinand Marcos. Estrada had neither formally resigned nor been dismissed. Withdrawal of military support for the President in face of popular outrage could set dangerous precedents. Notwithstanding the actions of President Estrada and eleven supporting senators in undermining confidence in democratic processes and the 'rule of law', in this case 'people's power' seems to have dangerously stretched the democratically endorsed 1987 Constitution.

More positively, Estrada's overthrow can be seen as evidence of Filipino democracy's resilience, despite some lack of constitutional punctiliousness in its manner of achievement. Overall, the Philippines appears to be progressing on both civil-political and socio-economic rights fronts. But doubts remain whether state institutions and ideology are strong enough to deal decisively with powerful oligarchic interest groups, and more recently Peronista style mass violence by Estrada supporters.

Previous emphasis on a 'strong state' as necessary to development has given way to a more confused neo-liberal outlook, in which privatisation has become the main weapon. Hutchcroft questions whether Filipino state institutions are capable of providing minimum political foundations for economic transformation, in supplying electricity and other vital infrastructure, protection from illegal logging, arbitrating business disputes, or even-handed regulation of the financial system. Liberal perspectives are also challenged by analyses emphasising democratic change of a kind which goes beyond institutions and processes to effectively confront structural links between class interests and state power.

Since President Ramos' election in 1992, the military has ceased to pose serious threats to civilian rule, although low level violence remains endemic across society. Crime and kidnapping, often involving the military have proved pervasive threats to human rights. Killing and kidnapping of journalists has further inflamed an environment of conflict and lawlessness. Truth here is confused by claims and counter-claims about the practice of journalists carrying arms either for self-protection or, in the view of critical colleagues, to act as self-appointed enforcers of justice or make money by obtaining additional gun licences.

Armed opposition, together with the state's response, still poses considerable threats to social stability and democratic order. The New People's Army (NPA), though weakened and divided, retains capacity to strike at the security forces in outlying regions, while urban guerilla groups are able to cause occasional disruption. The long-running Islamic insurgency appeared to have been settled in September 1996 when the Moro National Liberation Front (MNLF), signed a formal peace agreement. MNLF leader Misauri was subsequently elected Governor of the Autonomous Region of Moslem Mindanao (ARMM), covering four out of fourteen provinces which had given majority support. He also chairs the Southern Philippines Council for Peace and Development, which oversees the development of all (mostly Christian) provinces and cities. However, the MNLF's factional rival, the Moro Islamic Liberation Front (MILF) and other militant Islamic factions have continued the insurgency. Some have embarrassed the government with a series of kidnappings. Land issues, together with rising food shortages and population growth remain a central focus of conflict.

Residual violence in civil society and illegal use of state power and resources has created widespread popular disaffection, which threatens democratic consolidation and establishment of a political culture based on respect for universal human rights.

Thailand

Thailand avoided colonisation, unlike other Southeast Asian countries, enabling it to adapt to a changing external environment while maintaining continuity in its core institutions, centred on the monarchy and Buddhist religion. Thai monarchs were historically revered as absolute rulers, carrying a divine mandate. During the nineteenth century, a succession of reforming kings embarked on modernisation programmes, thereby creating a technocrat cum bureaucrat class and an increasingly powerful military. A military coup in 1932 replaced absolute with constitutional monarchy. But prior to the 1990s, political participation was confined to a limited elite. Thailand experienced thirteen constitutions, variously classified as democratic, non-democratic and semi-democratic, between 1932 and 1987, with thirteen general elections, sixteen coups, forty-three cabinets, sixteen prime ministers, of which six were military and ten civilian. While parliamentary institutions were invariably re-established, indicating their underlying legitimacy, constitutions were designed to serve the interests of their creators, usually by arranging for bureaucrats and military to join cabinets or exercise veto powers and influence via a Senate elected on a restricted franchise.

In a major push for democratic change in 1973, student demonstrations triggered the downfall of the military-led government. A new constitution and elections followed in 1975, but reform parties failed to win a clear majority. Extensive peasant and labour mobilisation alarmed conservative forces, leading to street clashes in Bangkok. Martial law was declared in October 1976, followed by a severe 'anti-communist' crackdown. This was relaxed one year later, following another coup by younger military moderates. Amnesty was offered to dissidents and a relatively liberal constitution promulgated in 1979, followed by elections. Military cooperation with democratic forces grew during the 1980s, under the leadership of General Prem Tinsulanond, though there were unsuccessful coups attempts in 1981 and 1985.

In 1988, Chatichai Choonhavan was elected as Prime Minister with a parliamentary majority, and Thailand finally seemed set on a firm course towards electoral democracy. But Chatichai was overthrown by a military coup led by General Suchinda Khraprayun in 1991, on the pretext of eliminating corruption. Following military dominated elections in March 1992, plans to install Suchinda as Prime Minister set off mass demonstrations, culminating in a violent crackdown by security forces in Bangkok in May 1992, in which over fifty people were killed. Following the King's intervention, Suchinda stood down and an interim government under the widely respected Anand Panyarachun pushed through constitutional changes. These required the Prime Minister to be an elected Member of Parliament (MP), and significantly reduced the powers of the Senate.

Thailand's 1997 constitution sets out principles of transparency, accountability and checks and balances between all arms of government, based on specification of their respective powers. The ninety-nine member Constitution Drafting Assembly (CDA), comprising one member from each of Thailand's seventy-six provinces plus legal and other experts, undertook extensive popular consultation. Its autonomy from political pressures and consequent legitimacy were enhanced by arrangements whereby Parliament could only approve or reject but not amend the draft, which was then put to popular referendum.

Persons assuming political office must declare assets and debts, lists of which must be publicly reviewed, checked and certified, both at the time of appointment and departure. Those giving false reports face five year bans and other penalties. One-fourth of members of the National Assembly can ask the Commission to investigate any of their number suspected of corruption, or may request the Supreme Court to launch a similar investigation against any Commission member.

The House of Representatives consists of 500 members, with 400 representing individual constituencies and 100 chosen under a party-list system on a proportional representation basis. In an attempt to reduce notorious party-switching, candidates on party lists must be party members. Senators are elected for six years and may not be re-elected to the next Senate term. The Senate's powers to delay either money or other bills have been effectively reduced to six months, though it has powers to seek information, express no confidence, and request investigations by judicial and other bodies. The King can delay Bills for up to ninety days. A two-thirds majority of the National Assembly is required to override his veto. Senators may not hold public office or be members of political parties. But indirect election as provincial representatives may enhance their influence.

Several elections between 1992 and 1998 were characterised by entrenched vote-buying, patronage and money politics. Elections in January 2001 also saw significant violence including widespread intimidation of canvassers. One apparent reason was increased pressure exercised by the National Counter Corruption Commission, using its new powers to deeply probe members from all parties. The Interior Minister under Chuan Leepkai was banned from politics for five years. One week prior to the 2001 elections, Thaksin Shinawatra, leader of the Thai Rak-Thai (Thai Love Thai) Party, was convicted of false assets declaration in 1997. His party subsequently retained an outright majority, following re-staged elections after the Election Commission had disqualified over fifty originally elected candidates. Thaksin has continued as Prime Minister pending appeal to the Constitutional Court.

Reflecting a widening economic gap, sharp differences in political culture and outlook have emerged during the 1990s between Bangkok, where democratic-oriented parties dominate, and much of rural and regional Thailand, particularly the impoverished north east, where traditional patron-client styles of politics persist, including direct vote-buying. The first stream, led by the Democratic Party under Chuan Leepkai, were broadly successful at elections in 1992 and 1998. This stream is viewed favourably in international business circles and has proved responsive to calls for economic and governance reforms. The second stream dominated under Prime Ministers Banharn and Chavalit following the 1995 election.

Thaksin's campaign in 2001 combined traditional patronage politics with new styles of populism. Widespread poverty, linked to slow economic recovery, generated impatience with the Leepkai government's 'dull' reform agenda, in sharp contrast with Thaksin's charisma, economic and cultural nationalist appeal. Many were prepared to regard his false assets declaration as a 'technical' error, hoping that as a multi-millionaire he would prove less vulnerable to corruption. Thaksin's overwhelming victory avoided the need to form a multi-party coalition - a long-standing cause of instability and corruption. Thus the popular legitimacy of Thai democracy and 'rule of law' imperatives may prove at odds, at least in the short term, as the Constitutional Court's pending ruling on Thaksin's case takes effect.

The Buddhist religion, while retaining its organisational and spiritual autonomy, has traditionally supported the social order, both directly through the Buddhist Sangha and by emphasising personal spiritual pilgrimage within a context of outward conformity to social customs and hierarchy, linked to values of harmony and non-competitiveness. Respect for authority is to be balanced by the powerful exhibiting moral virtue. While this traditional outlook tends towards pragmatic acceptance of the status quo, many monks preach against corruption, environmental destruction and materialist trends. There is also an individualist strand to Buddhist spirituality, which influences, for example, the formation of meditation and prayer sects among professional and business groups, which have in varying ways influenced the anti-corruption movement in Bangkok at the base of the democracy struggle in 1991-2.

The monarchy as an institution, particularly the present King Bhumipol, is deeply respected, even revered throughout Thai society, and disrespect to him is regarded as a near treasonable offence. The monarch has played crucial mediating roles in crises, supporting pro-democracy forces in 1973 and 1992, more moderate democratising versus right-wing military in 1981, though endorsing a military takeover in 1976. The continuing thread to his exercise of monarchical powers is the preservation of national unity. King Bhumipol is also pro-active in specific policy areas, notably rural development, local administration and environment, thereby forging closer rapport between the royal family and hill tribes.

The military's power appears to be finally waning after some sixty years of dominance. Military leaders have long assumed a 'guardian' role in upholding national identity and institutions, employing sweeping definitions of 'national enemies', commonly labelling pro-democracy activists as communists. While originally the major agent in limiting the king's powers, the military invariably claims to act in his name, though ultimately obliged to obey him. As in Indonesia, the military has played multiple modernising and developmental roles, including extensive involvement in economic enterprises. Its control over media is threatened by recent legislation. But internal disunity, linked to factionalism and shifting alliances with bureaucrats and parliamentarians, has limited scope for military dictatorship.

Concentration of administrative and economic power in Bangkok has resulted in dependence and lack of regional and local initiative. Effective transfer of resources will be crucial to successful outcomes.

Economic growth rates averaged above 8 per cent annually between 1980 and 1992. Gross National Product (GNP) per capita increased from US $810 to US $2110 over a decade from the mid 1980s, with life expectancy at birth reaching sixty-eight. Literacy rose from 50 to 90 per cent between the early 1960s and 1990s, with a rise in Thailand's HDI index from 0.465 to 0.798 between 1970 and 1992. Although 76 per cent were reported to have access to safe drinking water, more rapid investment in industrial relative to agricultural development, together with other 'urban-biased' public spending policies, continues to widen the urban-rural gap.

In recovering from the economic crisis, Thailand gained international confidence by supporting orthodox principles of economic management and good governance. At the same time, democratisation strengthened mobilisation by non-governmental groups. The Forum of the Poor organised many thousands of members to camp in front of government offices in Bangkok from late January until early May 1997 protesting government inaction on disputes involving land rights, problems of the urban poor, construction of dams and other projects resulting in loss of livelihood for farmers and fishermen. Proposed community forestry legislation generated further protest.

While evolution of democratic politics may ultimately lead to greater diffusion of citizen participation, party structures as yet lack popular roots and internally democratic organisation, with electoral competition based more on personalities than policy and ideology. Successful mobilisation by NGOs and other groups in support of the 1997 Constitution have caused some to regard them as the 'real opposition'. But others are sceptical towards NGOs acting as self-appointed representatives of the people without having to account for their actions. Independence from the political machinery enables them to undertake campaigns and initiatives impossible to others.

Labour groups have intensified pressures on both political and enterprise fronts. But despite a comprehensive new labour law enacted in August 1998, labour remains in a relatively weak position, worsened by the 1997 economic downturn. High levels of rural poverty cause a continuing influx of labour into Bangkok, swelled by migrant workers from more impoverished neighbouring countries such as Bangladesh, Cambodia, Laos and Myanmar. Around 600,000 are estimated to be working illegally, while the government wages running battles with 'people smuggling' syndicates.

Hewison has argued that business, and the middle class generally, remain ambivalent towards democracy, questioning its compatibility with political order and economic stability, with militant labour posing a special threat. However, regularised laws and mechanisms for arbitrating disputes are seen as essential to conducting globally-oriented business. Transition to democracy may thus be a convenient arrangement for ruling elites, without indicating ideological change. Though plausible, this thesis fails to account for the continuing upsurge of mobilisation outside the control of elites, whose divisions open up space for new groups to participate in the formal political sphere.

Has Thailand finally broken through to sustainable democratisation or will the present period prove to be yet one more phase in a cycle of semi-democratic cum authoritarian rule? Pessimists see corruption, electoral violence and money politics intensified during the January 2001 campaign, as aggravating the rich-poor gap, undermining Thailand's fragile democratic institutions, and reversing improvements in human rights. Optimists draw confidence from the survival and evident strengthening of democratic institutions during the post-1997 economic crisis, broadly-based social mobilisation and constitutional entrenchment of independent anti-corruption and electoral commissions. While the independence and integrity of these institutions has yet to be fully tested, the 1997 Constitution provides clear remedies for wrongdoing.

Thailand's long period of semi-authoritarian rule can be partly credited with sustained economic growth, but it also promoted uneven development and associated inequalities. Democratic consolidation requires broadening of support beyond the urban middle class, by addressing the needs of farmers, landless peasants, urban labour and minorities, and overcoming pervasive exploitation of women and children.

Democratic Consolidation in Southeast Asia

A comparative global study by Larry Diamond explores conditions under which democracy is likely to take root, with a primary focus on consolidating recently established democratic systems rather than their initiation. Over and above specific institutions, processes, and other supports, democratic systems need legitimacy. However great a constitution's philosophical appeal; citizens must be willing to defend it. This will depend greatly on perceived benefits, citizens' sense of ownership and potential alternatives.

To test the depth of democratic consolidation, Diamond proposes normative and behavioural indicators at the level of elites, organisations and the mass public. At the elite level, most significant opinion-formers, cultural, business and political leaders should uphold democracy as the best form of government, supporting constitutionally based laws and processes in their public comments and practice. In organisational terms, the right to pursue power by peaceful means should be mutually respected and illegal methods and incitement to violence and intolerance outlawed. At the popular level, a majority of at least 70 per cent should support democracy as the best system of government, with no more than 15 per cent actively preferring authoritarian models. No anti-democratic movement, party or organisation should enjoy a significant mass following, with little or no public tolerance of violent or illegal means of political expression.

Not a few western democracies would find difficulty in passing all these tests, although only fringe groups may transgress the behavioural requirements. In some western countries, the required 70 per cent positive belief in democracy could probably be achieved only in a negative sense, in terms of the late Sir Winston Churchill's adage that democracy is the worst system of government in the world, except for all the others. The USA struggles to attain a 50 per cent turnout at Presidential and Congressional elections, while scepticism towards politicians is pervasive in established democracies. Though partly due to conscious rejection of low standards, money politics and the like, much apathy is due either to lack of perceived relevance to personal interest, or to a more basic sense of alienation.

Consolidation in recently democratising countries is by no means an automatic process. Some may retain an empty institutional shell, with democratic norms and processes regularly violated, but with minimally free and fair elections held frequently enough to ward off external sanctions. Without systematic democratic deepening, embracing the whole gamut of regime performance, such states will sooner or later regress. The behaviour of state officials may enhance or weaken respect for democratic institutions, legal and constitutional processes, setting off correspondingly positive or negative cycles in the wider society. Economic performance is also salient in bringing credit or discredit on governments in areas of vital personal concern to citizens, even though its causal relationship with particular forms of government is problematic.

Diamond's model is salient in the currently volatile Southeast Asian context. Several countries are in highly uncertain states of transition. Among ASEAN's ten countries, the model appears most relevant to Thailand, the Philippines and Indonesia, which have recently gained or regained constitutional democratic institutions. There are apparently high levels of elite consensus favouring democracy in Thailand and the Philippines. Popular mobilisation supporting democratic values is strong in both countries, though institutions and processes remain threatened. Politicians are only partly responsive to demands from groups outside formalised political structures. With limited internal democracy, parties are based more on personalities than policy or ideology. The impact of corruption, violence and criminality on public life, particularly in the Philippines, remains the most serious systemic weakness in both countries.

Indonesia is difficult to categorise, having recently experienced its first broadly 'free and fair' election since 1955, but with the direction of constitutional and institutional reforms still uncertain and the future role of the military unresolved. Nevertheless, Indonesia has a long history of social and political mobilisation, based on widespread popular awareness, which proved major factors in overthrowing President Suharto. These participatory traditions will provide strong in-principle support for democratic institutions. But Indonesia's weak democratic culture, together with endemic corruption and poverty, is likely to sustain instability over many years.

Malaysia and Singapore articulate and practice their own unique brands of illiberal cum Asian democracy. Dissent and advocacy of alternative systems are marginalised in Malaysia, and virtually outlawed in Singapore. However, high electoral support for ruling parties is in large measure uncoerced. Malaysia has historically enjoyed high levels of party membership, particularly among Malays in both ruling and opposition parties. Sustained economic growth and relatively broad distribution of benefits has been impressive in Singapore and, until the 1997 downturn, in Malaysia also. There is no certainty that either country will move in the near future towards forms of democracy based on international standards of civil and political rights.

Cambodia appears most to resemble Diamond's empty shell example. Two national elections have been conducted under UN scrutiny during the 1990s, in a situation of extreme dependence on international economic assistance. Cambodia's institutions and processes threaten principles of democracy and human rights at every turn. But the traumas of the past three decades must always be borne in mind. Against that background, the limited extent of democratisation so far achieved could be considered encouraging.

Vietnam and Laos, as Communist one-party states, and Brunei under the benign but authoritarian rule of its Sultan, are at this stage obviously irrelevant to any assessment of democratic consolidation. Each are in their own way gradually opening to regional and international influences. Brunei is the second most economically prosperous country in ASEAN, but tolerates no kind of political dissent or even debate. Laos has tentatively begun the process of opening up its economy, with the Friendship Bridge across the Mekong river providing a direct road link with Thailand. Both Laos and Vietnam are cautiously following the Chinese road in seeking to combine capitalist development with continuing political monopoly by the Communist Party. Vietnam has an embryo democratic movement, though at this stage overshadowed by the strength of expatriate lobby groups. Although serious restrictions on civil and political rights continue, notably in relation to freedom of religion, Vietnam seems largely free from mass brutality against its population. The opposite applies in Myanmar, which evidences no plans for even minimal democratisation. But the strength of its democracy movement, and quality of leadership under Aung San Suu Kyi, will provide a strong popular support base when democratic systems are eventually established.

Diamond's model, by bringing civil society and associated modes of popular mobilisation into the picture, goes beyond Huntington's limited, process view of democracy. However, it falls short of the more globalised and multi-contextual concepts of Held, Falk and others canvassed in Chapter 1. It also tends to view economic and social aspects as instrumental to democratising objectives. Asian democracy paradigms pursue a reverse approach, adapting selected democratic elements to social, economic and state-building objectives.

3

International Protection of Human Rights

Introduction

The conception of human rights which we recommend can be made to transcend all differences in the subjectivities and practices of peoples, not merely across national-state lines, but as between the different arenas of the larger community. These images of the human rights enterprise have been principally generated in the West, evolving over time from the Enlightenment mind-set, including a confidence in the possibility of a rational social and political order based on individual rights that, over time, could facilitate progress and happiness for humankind as a whole. Underlying such convictions is a belief in the sufficiency of human reason, especially as it is manifested in science and technology, and a vestigial distaste for any intrusion on the terrain of human rights by recourse to religion, tradition, and emotion. The ideological foundations of this secularist approach are often implicit. Nevertheless, it tended to generate a cult of modernization that has for several centuries occupied center stage in the West. One result has been a dualism between progress and backwardness that has been damaging to non modernizing peoples.

On the other side of the debate, keeping in mind that these orienting observations are deliberate oversimplifications, one finds cultural relativists who take their cues from societal tradition, specific religious teachings, and the primacy of cultural settings. Such a position, often oblivious to plural and incompatible elements in cultural precept and practice, leads to an endorsement of the view that cultural attitudes automatically deserve deference and anything inconsistent that claims to derive from the international law of human rights has been either misinterpreted or can be disregarded. This position may also be accompanied by the ideological counterpoint in non-Western societies that alleged human rights standards are more properly understood to be disguised hegemonic claims by the West that, in a postcolonial era, are no longer entitled to respect and should more properly he repudiated.

As will be explained, both of these polar positions on the relevance of culture should be rejected. If the field of the protection of human rights continues to be controlled by these two interpretive perspectives in their various forms, the most probable result is a demeaning encounter between two forms of fundamentalism, the pitting of relentless secularists against hardened traditionalists.

The position taken here is that, without mediating international human rights through the web of cultural circumstances, it will be impossible for human rights norms and practices to take deep hold in non-Western societies except to the partial, and often distorting, degree that these societies or, more likely, their governing elites have been to some extent Westernized. At the same time, without cultural practices and traditions being tested against the norms of international human rights, there will be a regressive disposition toward the retention of cruel, brutal, and exploitative aspects of religious and cultural tradition.

One objective of normative standards is the protection of vulnerable individuals and groups from harsh forms of local prejudice that have hardened over time into custom and tradition and thereby achieved a kind of provincial legitimacy.

These two standpoints taken together suggest an intermediating relevance for both international law (standards, procedures, implementation) and for cultural hermeneutics, above all seeking to reconcile cultural and global sources of authority by reference to a core concern for the minimum decencies of individual and group existence. An emphasis on suffering and victimization provides indispensable guidance both in relation to gaps in international legal protection and to the task of distinguishing acceptable cultural orientations from unacceptable ones. Of course, the whole undertaking is complicated and contingent as different observers and experts will often disagree. What is sought, and must be relied upon in the end, is a dialogue about appropriate behavioral standards in an atmosphere of growing toleration for divergency arising from varying cultural identities.

One important consequence of the globalization of social, political, and economic life which often goes unnoticed is cultural penetration and overlapping, the coexistence in a given social space of several cultural traditions, as well as the more vivid interpenetration of cultural experience and practice as a consequence of media and transportation technologies, travel and tourism, cross-cultural education, and a logarithmic increase in human interaction of all varieties. Such a reality posits its own distinctive and opposing social demands: respect for *difference* (culture; to sustain diversity), acknowledgment of *sameness* (international law of human rights; to reestablish normative authority). The emergence and the implementation of international human rights embody both the opportunities and obstacles arising from this always-shifting interplay between the valuing of difference and the quest for sameness.

Such an interplay presupposes various interpreters and interpretations and, as such, has either produced controversy or led to the repression of one or more lines of interpreters and interpretations by the other on the basis of its greater power. A theme of this chapter is a bias in favor of controversy conversation or dialogue that expresses itself in political and social terms as a commitment to maximum political democracy. A vibrant society, on a global scale, is needed to ensure that democracy both engages the issues that affect lives and feelings and takes account of interdependencies. In effect, human rights and political democracy are symbiotically bonded.

It would be helpful to illustrate concretely the working out of this intermediation of culture and international law, and the reason why it seems a necessary and desirable enterprise. Consider what happens when intermediation is not undertaken. The neglect of the displacement and destruction of indigenous peoples reveals both a glaring oversight in the protection offered by the international law of human rights and the degree to which this corpus of authoritative law dedicated to the protection of all humans has itself been distorted by a modernization bias. The neglect of indigenous peoples is what might be described as an area of "normative blindness." It does not improve matters to contend that governments in non-Western cultural space have given their assent to the human rights framework embodied in an international law that is deficient in its treatment of indigenous peoples. First of all, virtually every government of a sovereign state, north or south, has adopted a modernization outlook that regards premodern culture as a form of backwardness to be overcome for the sake of the indigeneous. Proceeding on this basis, the preferred normative response to the existence of indigenous peoples is not deference to their cultural autonomy, but rather their orderly and equitable assimilation into the more benevolent and promising cultural space of the modernizing ethos. To the extent that international law offers any protection at all to indigenous peoples, it does so in an oblique and obscure manner that ineffectually purports to prohibit discrimination against individuals belonging to indigenous peoples and otherwise aims to remove those obstacles that prevent assimilation.

Such a deficiency in the protective framework, admittedly now being nominally challenged by recent initiatives, adds a dimension to this analysis namely, that for governments inhabiting non-Western cultural space there exists an important overlay derived from the reception of Western ideas and influence about statecraft and progress. In the name of development, indigenous peoples have been and are being destroyed and displaced in many parts of the Third World. Of course, such a process of displacement was virtually completed in the West by the middle of the last century. Such a deficiency in normative protection has been contested by counter traditions of thought within Western culture from the time of initial settlement in "the era of discovery," but with little success. The attempt to extend human rights protection to all individuals and groups within the orbit of sovereign authority, however, has been endorsed uncritically and universally. Even the cult of modernization has now been somewhat tempered and qualified to take account of the evident wish by many indigenous peoples to retain their autonomous cultural space as enclaves within the states that *resist* rather than *aspire* to assimilation into the encompassing cultural habitat of modernization.

This example of the fate of indigenous peoples as a subordinate culture victimized by a dominant culture suggests the relevance of exclusion and inclusion in evaluating the normative adequacy of human rights as a protective framework at a given time and place. Those *excluded* from rights-creating processes are only likely to be taken into account, if at all, in a partial and paternalistic manner. The achievement of more attention and understanding will depend on organized acts of defiance and resistance by those victimized peoples. This approach has hitherto been ignored by specialists in rights.

Exclusion from the rights-forming process is itself a denial of human rights, and is at best likely to produce unsatisfactory substantive results. The observation here is structural; to the extent that the international law of human rights is an exclusive result of the states system, it cannot hope to take account of the values and needs of peoples that are not adequately represented in that system or even constituted to qualify for membership. One factor that confirms this failure of coverage is the greater extension of concern as a state system has evolved in ways that have at least provided weak forms of representation for non state actors such as indigenous peoples. Indigenous peoples are an extreme instance, but the struggle of women, gays, children, ethnic minorities, and the poor for normative acknowledgment has also been agonizingly slow despite the pretensions of the West to uphold the dignity of the individual and to honor liberty of choice. Until pressed by agitation and movements from below, these vulnerable groups have only rarely, and then insufficiently, enjoyed legal protection from abuse. Neither the abstract promise of the cultural myth of toleration nor that of the positive legal order is sufficient. One role of a robust civil society is to overcome both normative and cultural blindness to human suffering. This raising of awareness requires deliberate efforts to counteract the vulnerability of previously excluded groups; lessening vulnerability in turn depends on developing inclusive forms of decentralized participatory democracy. As asserted earlier, democratization is both a vital precondition and a crucial ingredient of human rights protection.

Suppose, however, that contested cultural practices are democratically endorsed as beneficial. For instance, the Hindu practice of suttee may seem cruel to outsiders (and even to many insiders), but it is alleged by some to be a functionally necessary way to uphold the integrity of Indian family life. The cultural endorsement of suttee within Hinduism, however, is by now local and restricted and should not be exaggerated. Hinduism is rich in contradictory understandings of precept and traditions, and various Hindu evaluations of the status and duties of widows are tenable. Also, all cultures evolve in relation to experience, being influenced partly by intracultural and intercultural interaction, as well as through their participation and reflection upon wider normative frameworks, including that of human rights itself. In this regard, Hindu contact with the West, including its commitment to gender equality, alters Hinduism as a comprehensive belief system. These cultural revisionings flow in the reverse direction as well and have influenced the West's normative discourse on materialist values and relations with animals and nature. Cultural influence can also be regressive, as seen in the case of Eastern societies in relation to the environmental effects of an uncritical adoption of the cult of modernization.

Does human rights discourse take precedence over contrary cultural practices? I believe, together with many interpreters of the social and political scene, that taking suffering seriously is the Archimedes point for intermediation between the universal claim and the particular practice when it comes to resolving antagonisms between widely, endorsed human rights norms and culturally ordained patterns of behavior. R.B.J. Walker has aptly expressed this ethical disposition in the course of a more general examination of international relations: "The primary ground for ethical reflection no doubt remains a capacity to identify the intolerable." To be effective at local and community levels, the imposition of the universal must be by way of an opening in the culture itself, not by external imposition on the culture. Therefore, it is of great importance to nurture cultural rethinking, reinterpretation, and internal dialogue, an approach that is so powerfully and creatively embodied in the work of Abdullahi A. AnNa'im.

Can we ground this process of normative assessment on realities beyond the arbitrary and subjective? Is there a core enterprise of protection that relates to the individual and group experience of the species at a given stage of its biological evolution? One starting point for response is to set forth an enumerated list of practices that strike observers as "intolerable."

Rhoda Howard has recalled Barrington Moore's recital of "universal causes" of human misery as a way of validating core human rights claims:

- torture, or slaughter by a cruel enemy;
- starvation and illness;
- the exaction of labor by ruthless authorities in an exploitative manner;
- loss of beloved persons by the hostile action of others;
- rotting in prison, being burned at the stake, or losing means of subsistence as a result of expressing heretical or unpopular beliefs.

Such an enumeration identifies the territory of human suffering while leaving considerable latitude for interpretation, discussion, and even controversy. Walker offers an even more complex sense of the elements he associates with the intolerable:

- the devotion of resources to the extermination of the human species in whole or part;
- forms of economic development that bring extreme wealth to some while threatening the very survival of others;
- rapacious destruction of the planet for progress or profit;
- flagrant abuse of established human rights.

Walker cavalierly contends: "From the South Bronx to Beirut, from the proliferation of refugee camps to the persistence of apartheid, the intolerable is always visible to those who would nevertheless celebrate the achievements of the modern world."

I doubt whether Walker's sense of the intolerable is as widely, noticed or as visible as he supposes. His far-reaching contention goes beyond Moore's more intuitive enumeration in that much of what he would have us call "intolerable" is a hidden consequence of an essentially capitalist orientation toward nature and society that rests on the whole idea of modernity so central to the identity of and dominance by the West. In the language of this chapter, Walker is closely associating "the intolerable" with the historical negative consequences of what has been earlier referred to here as "the cult of modernization." The broader point being made here is not that this or that conception of the intolerable ought to be favored, but that a series of discourses on the nature of the intolerable as a method of deepening and extending discussion of human rights priorities and cultural obstacles can make a vital contribution to cultural intermediation and internal dialogue.

Such discourses may be of primary and most immediate benefit to activists, those animated to take action by conscience and compassion, engaged elements in civil society, that are seeking to promote reforms or safeguard vulnerable individuals or groups. The implementation of human rights is dependent on such interpretative work by activists but precisely where such efforts are most needed, their undertaking can be dangerous for the practitioners of interpretitive work.

An-Na'im refers to the 1985 execution of his mentor, *Ustadh* Mahmoud Mohammed Taha, in *Khartoum* in reaction to his exegetical work of normative reconstruction in relation to Islamic cultural practices and traditions. What Taha was doing cast doubt upon those elements of Islamic religious law, *Shari'a*, that are, in An-Na'im's, words "morally indefensible and practically impossible to maintain." What is proposed as corrective is liberating, and for that reason, threatening to the normative pretensions of those defending the status quo:

The author submits, as a Muslim, that God communicates through the social and physical environment as well as through the *Qur'an*, His literal and final word, and through the *Sunna*, traditions of His final prophet, Mohammed Ibn Abdillah. This Article contends that God's instructions must be understood and applied in light of all social and material phenomena.

An-Na'im's insistence that "a legitimate and lasting" solution "must develop from within Islam" places great responsibility on the scholarly capacity to interpret and persuade. As he acknowledges, the obstacles in real world circumstances are formidable: "Most Muslim scholars are either silent, in exile, or in prison." Elsewhere he confronts all even more difficult question as to whether authoritative cultural practices that inflict "intolerable" results and are more or less resistant to techniques of interpretative softening, can be overcome, or at least restricted in their application, by relying upon cross-cultural and intracultural reinterpretation.

Other efforts to find an interpretative foundation upon which to rest the basic quest for human rights deserve mention. These efforts, as with those of An-Na'im, often draw upon an enlarged and an enriched conception of culture and tradition, as well as try to bring religious energy directly to bear in a constructive manner. A recent document issued by a group of self-styled Third World Christians under the title "The Road to Damascus: *Kairos* and Conversion" is a fascinating contribution to this direction of human rights thinking, even though it is not so designated. I quote a passage that conveys the tenor of the whole:

God is on the side of the poor, the oppressed, the persecuted. When this faith is proclaimed and lived in a situation of political conflict between the rich and the poor, and when the rich and the powerful reject this faith and condemn it as heresy, we can read the signs and discern something more than a crisis. We are faced with a *Kairos*, a moment of truth, a time for decision, a time for grace, a God-given opportunity for conversion and hope.

This extension of liberation theology anchors human rights in the struggle against those forms of oppression afflicting especially the poor, and it entrusts the poor with a critical role as agents of their own liberation. It does not, in any sense, scorn political rights related to elections and representative democracy, nor does it rest its hopes on the fulfilling of economic rights conceived of as distinct claims, but rather it responds to an oppressive structure by issuing its own mandate to engage in collective resistance and transformative struggle, in effect suggesting that without a transformed social structure human rights will not be realized by the great majority of Third World peoples.

In introducing the very important collection of essays published recently under the title *Rethinking Human Rights*, editors Smitu Kothari and Harsh Sethi emphasize the critical importance they attach to moving beyond legalist and statist conceptions of human rights. They call for "a relevant *politics* of human rights," as well stressing the importance of "a human rights consciousness" which they believe is inhibited in Hindu India as a consequence of a lamentably passive attitude toward suffering, pain and death. Kothari and Sethi speculate:

> *Maybe we have lived with too much of them for too long. Mass death and suffering, we, as a society are keen to exorcise quickly. How else do we explain the near absence of a civic and humanitarian response to either the Bhopal disaster, or the subsequent governmental callousness? Nor are we, for that matter, very bothered about the thousands of hungry who swarm around us as beggars.*

They conclude, "None of this augurs well for human rights consciousness." In passing, it should be noted that cultural callousness is present in the West as well it does not take long to learn that in public places in the United States it is best to avert one's eyes from the often horrific spectacle of homelessness. By averting our eyes, we are keeping "the intolerable" at a safe distance; this usually results in societal indifference. Significant, here, is the enlargement of our understanding of "culture" to incorporate prevalent attitudes toward various forms of suffering, including the efforts of repressive, dominant, and exploitative elites to hide the costs of existing structures or to numb the sensitivities of the citizenry.

What I want to stress here is the recentering of the quest to implement human rights in the sinews of civil society. As such, cultural outlook becomes of transcending importance to the realization of human rights. It is less the crystalized abuses of state power that are of primary concern than the specific character of human suffering regardless of its source, and, as in the *kairos* document of Third World Christians, Kothari and Sethi call for "a social praxis, rooted in the need of the most oppressed communities, that seeks to create shared norms of civilized existence." Part of such rethinking involves the realization that waiting for the state and waiting for the United Nations are not nearly enough, even in situations in which one has a favorable view of those institutions.

The rethinking of human rights here proposed also entails a rethinking of culture itself. Reverting once more to Kothari and Sethi's approach, they note that India's cultural achievements, including the sustaining of democracy and her formal acceptance of human rights covenants as an ingredient of constitutionalism, are not enough, nor even is its leadership role in "the international struggle against colonialism, imperialism and racism," nor even its great fight to bring to the world "the message of 'nonviolence'":

> *Rarely do many of us realize, that underneath this impressive veneer and national pride about our 3000 year old civilizational legacy, lies a history of systematic violation of basic civil, democratic, and human rights of large sections of our population.*

India's cultural traditions, they argue, generate and are responsible, in various respects, for a significant portion of this oppressiveness; but the same culture, as they remind us, is also diverse enough to generate liberatory ethical and political possibilities. As with An-Na'im's approach to Islam, this Indian effort emphasizes, a root cultural/religious possibility of working within the Hindu framework for peace and justice, a possibility given historical plausibility by Gandhi's extraordinary exemplification of what Hinduism, reconstructed, could mean for all forms of social relations in the modern world. While An-Na'im emphasizes mainly doctrinal perspectives as a foundation for action, Kothari and Sethi (and their collaborators) call for social praxis, struggle, taking suffering seriously at the grassroots level of local and communal circumstances. The two standpoints are complementary, although their degrees of usefulness will depend on the context. India's social decentralization and severe communal tensions, together with the failure of the central state structure to exert influence on the tradition-bound countryside, commends an emphasis on activism. Islam's reliance on dogmatic applications of doctrine commends an emphasis on exegesis.

Kothari and Sethi believe that the international protection of human rights comes about through the activation of civil society. The most effective type of activation depends on the circumstances of time and place. As developments of recent years in Eastern Europe, especially Poland, suggest, the promotion of human rights there became almost exclusively a project of nonviolent movements of opposition and resistance, remarkably courageous jand sustained movements directed toward the nonviolent, yet militant, transformation of state power. Again, a legalistic understanding of the international protection of human rights could not provide much insight, especially as oppressor governments had previously mechanically and unproblematically accepted international human rights covenants, presumably believing that their firm domination of societal behavior by party and state made the commitment to uphold such standards of conduct irrelevant to the stability of internal control of the populations living in these countries.

At another level, these acknowledgments of legal obligation became important, although unwittingly, as they called the attention of the citizenry to the gap between rhetoric and performance that underscored and objectified the illegitimacy of these governments on their own terms, and the corresponding legitimacy of popular struggle for reform. In the end, it was the cultural resources which survived totalitarian assault, gave decisive strength and direction to these movements of resistance, and provided support and guidelines on a day-to-day basis. This was especially true of the religious institutions and traditions that acted as main legitimating sources of inspiration. Often, as in Poland, these elements of cultural heritage could themselves be historically associated with oppressiveness; the point, however, is that virtually any cultural heritage is morally rich enough that it can, if appropriately construed, under some circumstances make inspirational contributions to the struggle for human rights, democracy, and social justice. The international protection of human rights cannot proceed very far without liberating the culture itself to serve these ends.

The protection of human rights is hindered by the prevailing structure and organizational features of international society, especially the persisting predominance of a sovereign state. A built-in tension exists between the structure of international society and the effective implemenration of international standards of human rights. True, governments representing states and their population to varying degrees have accepted human rights standards directly or indirectly, but many governments also violate these norms, often in systematic and extreme ways. Of course, even nominal adherence to human rights standards reduces the weight of purely sovereignty-oriented arguments, thus giving international public opinion, including diplomatic interchange, a plarform to stand on. Even here, it is less the state structure than the array of transnational voluntary associations (NGOs) that have exposed human rights failures. Most states, even when avowedly concerned about human rights, often lack capability and credibility, having too much to hide themselves and generally subordinating and eroding the credibility of their human rights concerns by according priority to geopolitics.

Such selectivity in protest activity introduces an element of hypocrisy and manipulativeness into most statist (and even international institutional) approaches to human rights. There are some notable exceptions, for instance, the Scandinavian group: countries that have a decent record on human rights at home and take pains to keep their international concerns about human rights distinct from their geopolitical position and outlook.

World order thinkers have long noted that the state is both too big and too small it is too big in the sense that it can wield world-disruptive military power externally and that it loses ability to sustain a political community internally; it is too small in the sense that it cannot extend its authority for or effectively enough to control the flow of entropic forces in the world or to fashion suitable regimes for handling global scale problems. Human rights thinkers might well conclude that the state is both too strong and too weak in relation to the protective enterprise it is too strong in the crucial respect that if it is the source of gross violations, it becomes exceedingly difficult, if not impossible, to organize effective opposition, at least in the short run; it is too weak in the equally crucial respect that, even when disposed to implement human rights standards internally, it can only rarely and marginally overcome contrary cultural practices, especially if these are deeply ingrained and widely dispersed. The irony can be expressed as a paradox: only a totalitarian state could hope to realize human rights fully in a fundamentalist culture, but by being totalitarian it would stake out an identity that would necessarily be antagonistic to basic human rights. In contrast, several, but by no means all, human rights NGOs have achieved a measure of influence because of their single minded dedication to human rights without regard to the ideological identity, and political alignment of the state accused of violating human rights. Their information on human rights abuses is difficult to refute or dismiss on the grounds of bias or partisan politics.

Yet another element must enter into consideration: political power tends to be distributed territorially. An oppressive state, while possibly even the object of intense censure, generally remains master of its domestic scene until challenged from below and within that is, by aroused societal forces that, though they may involve international law as their justification, are mainly motivated by values and experiences associated with domestic, cultural, and political reality. Of course, arenas external to the state can participate and contribute, as the anti-apartheid campaign so well illustrates. Still, such external pressure has marked limits, enabling a tiny and isolated Albania, for example, to disregard international pressure for decades. Bypassing the state can be extraordinarily important to counteract domestic oppression. The reorientation of cultural consciousness such as Gandhi attempted so heroically in India, can directly challenge oppression at its communal and behavioral roots. Whether Gandhi's link between justice and nonviolence is indispensable in this process of cultural renovation is far from evident and undoubtedly depends on the specific context, it is true. At the same time, it is certainly notable that widely disparate popular struggles for human rights and democracy during the 1980s have rejected violence as a means, or at least as a principal means, for pursuing their ends. One thinks immediately of democratization initiatives in Eastern Europe and the Soviet Union, but also of the "people power" in the Philippines that drove Ferdinand Marcos into exile, of the Chinese student movement so brutally crushed in June of 1989 on Tiananmen Square and of the Palestinian *intifada*.

In the end, the protection of human rights is not distinguishable from the struggle for democracy and decency in the world, and may not long be separable from the repudiation of the cult of modernization in the West. The Greens (and those who are working to re express the religious affirmation of feminine sacred energy as pervading earthliness) are bringing back into the cradle of Western civilization a normative questioning that is itself subversive (of the supposed cultural mainstream. It is not surprising that Matthew Fox, a Dominican theologian who reinterprets the Christian message under the sway of ecofiminism, has been silenced for a year by Cardinal Joseph Ratzinger, the chief Vatican guardian of orthodoxy.

My conclusion is that the prospects for human rights are linked to the prospects for cultural reconstruction and that these prospects depend upon an open process of communication, free from dogmatic interferences. It is only from within the spiritual and humanistic core of civil society that restorative energies can emerge to redress cultural imbalances. History, may move, but global circumstances are exceedingly uneven. The core of human rights is one thing for the Kairos group, another for Solidarity in Poland, still another for Indians beset by menacing communal violence, another for those seeking to perpetuate and protect the cultural forms of indigenous peoples and still another for the ecologically threatened West. It is Ironically appropriate that the birthplace of modernity should also be most audibly in its death throes in this period. Europe 1992 is a continuation of the cult of modernization in a more efficient form of larger aggregations of capital; but it is also a stimulus to ecological consciousness, proceeding by way of reorienting territorially based geopolitics. The electoral success of the Greens in Europe is, above all, an indication of deep cultural ferment, including a very different fix on what upholding human rights entails from the orientation implied in the Enlightenment.

My closing self indulgence as to offer a few comments on the affair of Salman Rushdie that follow from the preceding analysis. Let me stake a small personal claim. I am probably one of very small number of wanderers on this planet that has had the experience of a personal meeting with both Rushdie and his now deceased adversary, Khomeini. Reduced to essentials, the turmoil generated by the publication of *The Satanic Verses* cries out for careful reflection from many distinct angles. To begin with, Khomeini's reaction was grounded in a widespread Islamic sense that Rushdie's novel exceeded the boundaries of literary convention, that it was deliberately, provocative by scandalizing the Prophet Muhammad and his associates. Of course, the glory of Western liberty is based on protecting precisely those forms of expression thus castigated at the time of their utterance; but such an achievement itself depends on what might be called "cultural preparation," which is definitely not present at this time in the Muslim world. Put differently, human rights enshrined in international law, and largely embodied in Western cultural practice, cannot be effectively protected in some cultural settings. Indeed, their attempted implementation may produce a devastating breakdown of social order as well as a heightening of influence for restrictive or fundamentalist cultural tendencies

Rushdie's novel also illuminates the problematics surrounding the territorial organization of the contemporary world. Although published in the West, the book (and its outlook) quickly penetrated the Muslim world. Indeed, there were riots in India, Pakistan, and elsewhere in reaction to the book weeks before Khomeini issued his infamous death sentence (which was backed up by a huge monetary reward for the prospective assassin). At the same time, Khomeini by his own decree effectively "killed" Rushdie as a normally functioning citizen in a democratic society; nothing the West could do by way of territorial law or moral protest has enabled Rushdie to continue fully with his life as a public man of letters, someone who had previously played an active role in English political and literary life giving readings around the world and taking controversial stands on policy issues. Even after Khomeini's death, Rushdie remains in deep hiding, possibly condemned to live underground for the rest of his life, or, at best, to live more openly but in a certain indeterminate jeopardy. Who can know the extent of risk that Rushdie would face if he emerged from hiding? The modern state, despite its military and police prowess, can be penetrated in many ways; it can no more give Rushdie protection against this onslaught of Islamic fundamentalism than it can insulate its borders against the influx of drugs, illegal immigrants, acid rain, the vagaries of financial markets, or "alien" ideas.

But there is another facet of *The Satanic Verses* that bears on my main theme. Insulating the sensitiveness of Islamic society against such provocations is not necessarily oppressive at the present time, and may well represent a prudent intervention by a ruler faced with the likelihood of riots. To condemn such governments by invoking international law and piously insisting upon unrestricted freedom of expression is to fall into the trap of secular fundamentalism, which can in its own way be as repressive of human dignity as Islamic (or otherwise religiously grounded) forms of fundamentalism. The Enlightenment conception of virtue is not necessarily prescriptive for non-Western peoples, although it has been largely entrenched in the positive law of human rights.

In addition, perhaps unrestricted artistic expression may even not yet be thoroughly grounded in the lifeworld of the West. Martin Scorsese's film *The Last Temptation of Christ*, offensive to many Catholics, exhilarating to many others (including Catholics), induced boycotts and bomb scares at theaters. One can only speculate about what violence might have ensued had the Pope encouraged Catholics to take all means to prevent the showing of the film and backed the injunction with huge financial rewards. From the perspective of democratic values, it would invariably seem desirable to open up a culture as far as imaginable to enable diverse viewpoints to be freely expressed and debated. Of course, the option of a culture to minimize out side influence and intrusion cannot be always ruled out. Assessment depends on context. Small tribal peoples, for example, might opt for insulation in a spirit that outsiders should generally respect, especially if the tribes' cultural practices did not involve deliberate cruelty or universally condemned abuses such as torture.

Toleration is the positive reverse side of orthodoxy and fundamentalism, but the problems of repressiveness should not be superciliously posited in non-Western cultures such as Islam, whose interests can then be ignored as unworthy of concern. Also, the abuse of artistic freedom to deride vulnerable peoples, or worse, to stimulate harm against them, is culturally problematic and ambiguous even from a human rights standpoint. For instance, literature or films that evoke hatred of minorities or vulnerable groups, and which might lead to abuse and violence, present difficult choices for leaders. Only secular fundamentalist attitudes toward human rights can resolve such issues at the abstract level of human rights standards. As such, the one-sidedness of the reaction to Rushdie's plight in the liberal West must be understood, in part, as a continuing expression of what Edward Said has so convincingly portrayed as "Orientalism," the negative stereotyping in the West of Islam leading to dreadful consequences for the Palestinias and others. Many of those who were most "outraged" by Khomeini's response to *The Satanic Verses* have also been outspoken opponents of justice for the Palestinians.

In the end, I think, we can most successfully uphold human rights by struggling against "the intolerable" in all its forms. We must make full use of our ingenuity and democratic opportunities to discuss what is intolerable, trusting in freedom of communication to be itself clarifying and hence liberating. As such, *human rights, cultural renewal,* and *participatory democracy* are implicated, for better or worse, in a common destiny.

But suppose there is no democratic possibility? As recent decades have shown, authoritarian repression of media, intellectual life, and cultural expression drives freedom of communication underground, although it cannot abolish it. Whether by *samizdat*, satire, or humor, the voices of dissent manage eventually to tind arenas and forums, although not without risk, often with the help of religious institutions that under other circumstances have themselves exerted their influence to restrict the dissemination of dangerous knowledge. Even in Iran, it was the mosque that mainly kept alive the possibility of democratic questioning of the Shah's repressive political order during the twenty-five years of dynastic rule. It is not plausible to imagine the triumph of Solidarity and democratization in Poland without the earlier inspirational support given by the Catholic Church, an institution so notable in Polish history for playing the opposite role There are no fixed points of normative reference, so that we are all responsible for the discovery and protection of human rights, and must establish such a process of inquiry as to be itself an expression of the integrity of any given cultural identity.

4

Human Rights Law in Global World

Introduction

The breakup of the CSFR into two independent states as of January I993 indicates, among other things, that the same legal-political process will need to be redone for the Czech Republic and Slovakia. This bifurcation of Czechoslovakia, ending a nation-state of some seventy years duration, reflects the implementation of the collective human right of peoples to self-determination. Whether in Slovakia this collective right leads to the reaffirmation of internationally recognized individual rights, and of minority rights for ethnic Hungarians, was not clear at the time of writing.

When one focuses on codification and implementation of legal standards (even if at an earlier stage of analysis these standards are considered moral ones), it is well to emphasize at the start that the respect for human rights within any state cannot be assessed apart from the larger sociopolitical context (with economics understood as a social factor). Thus, we must consider legal standards of human rights not in the abstract but in relation to the national society, the region, and the international system in which they exist.

Keeping this broad perspective in mind, we find that in the three states under review the development of respect for human rights manifested certain aspects in common. At the same time, however, there were marked differences. Ultimately, we shall find both problems and progress concerning the condition of human rights in this part of the new Europe.

Political Culture and Human Rights Codification

Historically speaking, one can say that all three of these states represented a connecting link between East and West. In their historical development the influence of Western and Eastern cultures mingled, but not in exactly the same way in each. In our opinion, Western influences were greater in the CSFR and Hungary and lesser in Poland. This has relevance for the fate of human rights today.

In another chapter, Bruce Garver notes the democratic tradition in the CSFR, a tradition stronger than in the other two states. While Professor Garver notes that this tradition had its weaknesses, neither Hungary nor Poland can match the practice of civil and political rights in Bohemia, Moravia, and Slovakia during the period of the first republic (1918-38). There was also a democratic tradition in Bohemia, Moravia, and Silesia in the second half of the last century and in the beginning of this one under the Habsburg monarchy. In particular, some democratic political parties flourished during this era.

Fewer comparable features can be found in Hungary and Poland, although there were of course some democratic movements. These were, for the most part, either short-lived or aborted at the start. At the same time, as Professor Garver notes, one should not overestimate the strength of the democratic tradition of the CSFR. At a minimum, one should note forty-two years of recent authoritarian rule centered in Prague, as well as the fact that this authoritarian rule was supported or tolerated by much of the population. Thus, reference to the CSFR's democratic tradition may now entail more political rhetoric than ingrained belief in genuine democratic values. It remains to be seen whether an independent Czech Republic proves more democratic than a Slovak Republic. The Slovak Republic during World War II was decidedly authoritarian.

It may be that some believe the Anglo-American phrase "rule of law" accentuates its procedural aspects, whereas the continental phrase "state according to law" captures the full substance. This argument need not detain us here.

The Charter of Basic Rights and Freedoms in the CSFR did not, unlike the Spanish and Portuguese constitutions, explicitly mention the rule of law. Nevertheless, the CSFR charter specified a rather detailed rule of law pertaining to human rights, for example, by stating that legal restrictions on rights must be equally valid for all cases of common characteristics. It would have been desirable, however, to provide wording similar to that in the Fundamental Law of Germany, which states: "In no case shall the basic right be violated in its nature". Also, the CSFR charter did not prohibit ex post facto laws or bills of attainder, as does the U.S. Constitution.

The CSFR charter also addressed the question of the relationship between a national rule of law and international law. For the c s F R, it was clear that treaty law to which the state has consented was, if we use the wording from the U. S. Constitution, the supreme law of the land, generally obligatory in state territory and superior to statutes. Unfortunately, the CSFR charter did not codify the basic principles from international human rights law. Efforts to this end by the Czechoslovak Helsinki Committee proved unavailing. For the time that the CSFR existed, and if we assume that the new constitutional court functioned, it would have been able to judge the legality of statutes and subsequent regulations in terms of whether they complied with the charter and the charter is basically consistent with the international law of human rights. At least in theory this was a very positive development, for national law was reinforced by international law.

In Poland, there was also no general statement about the rule of law, but there was a statement that Polish provisions on human rights must be interpreted consistently with the 1948 United Nations Universal Declaration of Human Rights, and with the human rights treaties to which Poland has consented. There was a comparable statement that the international law of human rights should be understood to be superior to national statutes. Such was the Polish commitment to rights that there was a statement providing for a change in the constitution if that legal instrument comes to be at variance with a human rights treaty accepted by Poland in the future. It can be seen, therefore, that democratic Polish leaders tried to secure rights by giving great prominence (and legal status) to international law, in the event that some future Polish government were inclined to violate nationally enumerated rights.

In Hungary, the draft revised constitution referred to the "transition to the State according to Law," and to a "democratic State according to Law." There was also reference to the need for conformity between national and international law.

Hungary revised Chapter XII of its 1949 Constitution in order to advance human rights; in so doing it formulated many rights in absolute rather than limited or relative terms. The same was true in Poland in late 1991. This absolutist approach pertained to freedom of speech, information, press, and assembly. On the surface, this development bore resemblance to that of the communist period, in which formulation of rights was also absolutist. Whereas the communists relied on practice to *negate* the rights, Hungary and Poland may rely temporarily on practice to *limit* the rights. Eventually it will be desirable to limit these rights through detailed and explicit qualifications, as has occurred in the long-standing democracies.

In the CSFR, the charter allowed for restriction on the basis of the rights of others, state security, public security, and protection of public health and morality. Property rights could also be restricted. In Poland, constitutional language of a similar nature was debated, both regarding general rights and property rights. Poland is likely to allow restrictions on the basis of either public order or infringement on rights of others. Hungary, too, debated similar language for similar reasons.

In fact, all societies restrict rights in certain situations and for certain reasons, and the balance between rights and their restriction is always problematical. Particularly on the question of rights versus national security, we believe that a useful test is whether the threat to national security presents "a clear and present danger," as that concept is used in U. S. constitutional law. Nevertheless, it must be admitted that what is a clear and present external danger, and what is a genuine internal threat to public order, or what is an overriding right of another, is always a difficult issue to resolve with general wording.

Theoretical and Technical Aspects

In all three states discussed here, the theoretical basis of legal codification is the same namely, natural law. This basis marked a change from the communist period. During that time, it was only possible in public papers to refer to natural law indirectly and despite a certain risk, by arguing that the fundamental right to life was based on natural law, from which flowed all other specific rights. The decline of communism allowed the three states to resurrect both natural law and legal positivism from the earlier German and Austrian practice, which fits with prevalent legal theories in Western democracies including those that influenced the European Convention on Human Rights.

Basing human rights on natural law can be deduced from both the CSFR charter and the Hungarian draft constitution. In the Polish draft constitution there were explicit references to natural law. In both Poland and Hungary, natural law is emphasized by a number of legal scholars, and in the latter state some court judgments rely on natural law.

Beyond a common basic theory, each state manifested different technical aspects inherent in the codification of human rights, as moral rights were formalized into legal rights. In the CSFR charter, there were six chapters, sometimes subdivided further. This technical framework was not altogether satisfactory, as there was considerable confusion over whether one right or set of rights was more fundamental than another. During the drafting process, a number of critics pointed out ambiguity concerning whether there were *fundamental* freedoms, from which specific rights flowed, and whether all rights and freedoms were on an equal footing. Thc latter view was articulated in reference to the international law of human rights, which was supposed to affect human rights law in the CSFR. It was possible to argue, on the basis of the charter's wording and organization, for example, that political rights were not really basic. This author prefers a well thought-out framework based on a natural law hierarchy, starting with the right to life. But the technical aspects of the c s F R charter allowed neither this argument nor a clear argument on behalf of equality of all rights. That being the case, clarity would only have arisen from judicial interpretation.

The technical aspects of the Polish draft constitution, both as devised by an expert committee and by the Senate, were far more adequate, since there was an early statement of general principles, followed by individual and personal rights, followed by economic, social, and cultural rights. There are minor differences between the two versions.

Finally in this section, we should note that the CSFR listing of rights was quite lengthy, and that more brevity would probably have been desirable. Likewise, Hungary started to list in detail the national codification of extensive specific rights derived not only from the Universal Declaration of Human Rights and the related United Nations covenants, but also human rights provisions derived from the Helsinki Accord of 1975 and related documents from the process called the Conference on Security and Cooperation in Europe (CSCE). Poland, on the other hand, at least by the early I990s, did not go into as much detail. It should be recalled that the U. S. experience with a brief statement of rights principles, amended only rarely over the years, has been a good one, although the constitutions of its internal states have been just the opposite lengthy and often amended.

Types of Rights

In general, all three states recognized the same rights as found in international law, both global (e.g., UN-derived) and regional (e.g., derived from the Council of Europe). In the following discussion, we are aware of the difficulty of using the traditional international practice regarding the grouping of rights. While it makes some sense to speak of the difference between civil and political rights, for example, the two categories can be merged as in the right of peaceful assembly and the right to freedom of speech. Nevertheless, the traditional groupings are useful for an organization of the analysis.

All three states recognized extensive individual civil rights, such as the right to life, the inviolability of the person, the right to privacy, exclusion of forced labor, the right to private property, freedom of movement, freedom on conscience and religion, and the right to intellectual property. There were also extensive rights to judicial due process, and there was an exhaustive listing of these in the CSFR charter. The lengthy specification concerning due process rights may reflect concern about their absence in the preceding communist period.

For similar reasons there was considerable attention to property rights in all three states. However, the CSFR charter stated that property rights could be overridden by concern for human health, nature, and the environment. Also in Hungary great attention was paid to property rights, and it was stated in the draft constitution that expropriation of private property had to be an exceptional matter only, and against compensation. The situation was the same in Poland.

As for political rights, all three states provided the usual catalog of these rights, such as freedom of assembly, the right of association, the right to petition, the right to form political parties. There was attention to voting rules, which are entirely consistent with West European practice. (On this subject see the chapter by John Hibbing.) Poland provided relatively more reference to referenda than did the other two states, although the CSFR codified recourse to a referendum on collective self-determination.

The CSFR charter contained an unrealistic provision on the full separation of political parties from the state. This, again, is a reaction against the party-state combination of the communist period, but since political parties organize the operation of the state, they can hardly be fully separate from it. While the Italian and German constitutions refer to political parties, it is clear that parties organize those states, and that one can have both free political parties and a close linkage to the state. The democratic intent of the Hungarian draft constitution was clearly expressed: "Political parties must not exercise public power directly. In accordance with this provision no political party may control separately any organ of the State".

All three states endorsed the notion of social, economic, and cultural rights. In this position they are consistent with the democratic states of Western Europe, but not with the United States. This position conforms to the international law of human rights. It is well to note that in the CSFR and Poland, these rights clearly had an inferior status compared to individual civil and political rights. The situation was significantly different in Hungary. In the Hungarian draft constitution one found a lengthy list of socioeconomic rights, which seemed to be on a par with civil and political rights. That legal instrument referred to the following rights: to work, to just and satisfactory working conditions, to compensation that is appropriate to the work performed and to a free and dignified life for himself or herself and for the family, to rest and regular holidays, to adequate health, to labor safety, to adequate medical attention, to social security, and to unavoidable unemployment compensation.

Cultural rights were most important in the CSFR, where a portion of the Slovak people for a time asserted their rights in cultural, as well as political, terms, as Pavel Hollander notes in his chapter. To conclude this section, one can say that all three states built on the concept of a natural law theory of human rights—in a technically detailed way.

One might wish that certain formulations and frameworks had been done differently, but this should not obscure the clear effort to define and implement human rights in a way familiar to all Western democracies.

One can add, however, that this effort at codification should not, as the British say, become a set of revered rules, but rather an institutionalized and functional process to guarantee human dignity. One can initially focus on codification, but this should be followed by political and sociological studies dealing with policies and attitudes. Legal rules do not implement themselves. One must monitor the political culture that, in the last analysis, accounts for implementation of rights. This is especially important after some forty years of authoritarian governance, regardless of how sound the theoretical basis and technical formulation of human rights might be in democratically fashioned legal instruments. The "law in action" and not the legal texts will be the basic indicator of the implementation of human rights in the life of a society.

In this regard, it should be noted that the legal drafting of the CSFR Constitution and human rights charter, which was of reasonably high quality, did not prove an effective barrier to the disintegration of the state. An emotional ethno-nationalism on the part of some in Slovakia, which in turn provoked independent movements in the Czech lands, made much legal drafting either irrelevant or redundant.

Organizational Guarantees

The judicial interpretation of the Constitution, whatever the precise legal rules of the process, forms an integral part of both democracy and the rule of law. (Some democratic states, such as Britain, differ on this point, in that they do not provide for judicial review of legislative acts to test for conformity with the [unwritten] constitution.) There are three basic models for judicial interpretation of constitutional rights. The first is represented by the United States, in which the U. S. Supreme Court rules on general legal questions and has the ultimate say on constitutional rights. The second is a special constitutional court that does not have general jurisdiction on non constitutional questions. Germany, Austria, and Italy, among others, manifest this phenomenon. The third is the hybrid model, in which a special chamber of a more general court handles constitutional questions. Switzerland is a good example of the hybrid model.

For the three continental European states under review in this chapter, adopting a specialized constitutional court was a matter of course. Czechoslovakia had copied the Austrian model prior to 1938. During the brief Prague spring of 1968, a similar court, but more along the lines of the German example, was projected but never actualized. In I99I the CSFR again adopted a constitutional court. Hungary and Poland also moved toward a constitutional court after the political revolutions of 1989.

Despite some technical variation in the three states, the overall organizational guarantees of constitutional rights were similar. Poland anticipated a slight variation, as the new constitutional court there showed a preventative competence to rule on draft bills before they became law. It seems that Poland looked to the French Constitutional Council as a model on this point. Such a preventative or anticipatory ruling was expressly prohibited in the CSFR. Also, since the CSFR was a federal state, the federal Constitutional Court exercised some authority over the two constituent republics; this was obviously not the case in more centralized Hungary and Poland. In the latter two states, the Constitutional Court could initiate proceedings, whereas in the CSFR, proceedings were to be initiated by the parties to a legal dispute.

There were a number of differences concerning the membership of these constitutional courts, but these details need not detain us here since they are not particular to human rights.

It seems well established that in all democracies operating under the rule of law, a principal part of constitutional interpretation involves protection of human rights. This seems particularly true in the specialized models, which deal only with constitutional questions. The willingness of citizens to bring individual complaints, combined with the orientation of the judges and indeed the legal traditions of the country, affect the organizational protection of human rights considered to be one of the most important factors.

An important issue for the judicial protection of human rights is whether the constitutional and other courts of a state will use international law directly to resolve a human rights claim. In the United States, for example, courts may or may not use a treaty directly in national court proceedings (whether in federal or state courts), depending on which treaty and/or which legal issue is before the court. Courts in the United States have on occasion used international customary law directly in a case. In the United Kingdom, as a general rule, courts will not use a treaty directly but must have, under the doctrine of incorporation, an act of parliament supplemental to the treaty before courts will accept jurisdiction over a claim based initially on international human rights law (or any other part of international treaty law).

In the three states considered here, international treaties on fundamental human rights and freedoms ratified and promulgated by the state CSFR, Hungary, and Poland were universally binding on their territories and superseded national laws. Guarantees of fundamental rights and freedoms were realized by constitutional courts and not, as noted in the example of the United States, by common courts using treaty law directly.

Beyond constitutional courts, we should note that since administrative rules must also be in conformity with the constitution, in all three states administrative courts could refer to the human rights codified in the constitution in their administrative rulings.

Even if we emphasize the role of judicial interpretation of basic rights, we should also note the use of the office of ombudsman. Both Hungary and Poland wrote such offices into their draft constitutions. This was not the case in the Cs FR. In the former two states, it was clear that the ombudsman was expected to try to achieve a non-juridical solution of various human rights problems.

Summary

In the Cs FR, Hungary, and Poland, the creation of a legal system for the protection of human rights marked a departure not only from their communist periods, but also from the legal systems of other former communist states that have been hesitant about the legal protection of human rights. The constitutional law framework, including organizations for interpretation, closely resembles constitutional and judicial arrangements in that part of Europe which has manifested democracy and pluralism for a considerable time. While there may be some need in the future to adjust existing and emerging rules and agencies in a minor way, the larger and decisive question is the extent to which the human rights values codified in the laws of the state, which are basically consistent with international law, will become consensual norms intrinsically accepted by a large element of the population. The breakup of Czechoslovakia underscores the need to address these same legal-political questions in the two emerging republics.

5

U. S. Policy for Human Rights

Introduction

It is not surprising that some truly remarkable events have taken place things that are very difficult for the average American to understand. Indeed, the democratization process has given new meaning to the old adage that truth is stranger than fiction.

Take, for example, the case of tiny Bosnia-Herzegovina. The former Yugoslavian internal republic has declared its independence, joined the United Nations, and become front page news because of a combination of war and human rights violations committed by various parties. According to the Bosnian constitution, the seven-member collective presidency a presidency that is democratically elected by the people must have two Serbs, two Moslems, two Croats, and either a Yugoslavian or a Gypsy. The attempts to address ethnic diversity were ultimately unsuccessful, but it clearly demonstrated the problems of building states.

Another example was the remarkable events that the democratic revolution unleashed during the first election in the Czech and Slovak Federative Republic. One of the competing parties was the Democratic Forum, which ran on a human rights ticket individual liberties, due process, respect for the rights of the accused, and the like. What made this party remarkable was that it was composed entirely of diehard Communist party members. Their human rights platform was motivated in no small part by a desire to avoid prosecution for past abuses.

The Democratic Forum is not the only remarkable political party to emerge in the wake of the Velvet Revolution. Other political parties included the Friends of Beer and the Erotic Initiative party. While these examples are obviously the exception rather than the rule, they do highlight the fact that progress in human rights and democratic pluralism will follow its own unique course in Eastern and Central Europe.

This chapter will focus, first, on the manner in which the United States has responded to the democratization process and in particular what Congress is doing to support the process. Second, it will briefly outline where the countries of Eastern and Central Europe fit into the overall U. S. foreign aid effort and the role of democratization within the U. S. SEED (Support for the Eastern European Democracies) Program. Finally, this chapter will conclude with some comments on the lessons learned, which might help these reemerging countries make the transition to democracy less difficult.

The General Setting

In October 1989 the House Foreign Affairs Subcommittee on Human Rights and International Organizations, where I serve as the ranking Republican, held a series of hearings on human rights in Eastern Europe. Those hearings focused on the widespread arrests of human rights activists which were occurring as governments sought in vain to maintain absolute control. In October 1989 the Berlin Wall was still very much of a reality, and people like Eric Honecker in East Germany and Nicholae Ceausescu in Romania were insisting that history would vindicate communism. During the subcommittee hearings, we received testimony from a wide range of individuals and organizations concerned with the arrest or harassment of religious leaders and human rights activists. The subcommittee's goal at the time was primarily to heighten international awareness of the arrests in hopes of facilitating the release of some of the political prisoners rounded up by these dictators in their desperate efforts to remain on top. Thus the emphasis in the subcommittee was on liberalization and not on democratization. Yet, within a few short months, communist dictators had been rounded up in many parts of the region. Now, many of those political prisoners are leading new governments. For example, the people of East Germany selected a dissident Lutheran pastor to lead the movement toward reunification with West Germany. Czechoslovakia, of course, chose the playwright Václav Havel to lead their newly democratic nation. The Hungarian president was a noted poet, and the first president of one of the newly liberated Baltic states was a dissident professor of music. While students of politics should be heartened by and even joyous about the advances in human rights, civil liberties, pluralism, and democracy, we must also approach this issue with a sense of realism. No democracy has been bom without strife and confusion. Nor is it the case that revolution automatically results in freedom and democracy. Clearly, even violent revolution in Romania has not brought democracy to that most troubled nation. The nations of Central and Eastern Europe have some of the attributes of democracy, while some commonly recognized liberties are in the process of being institutionalized. Other fundamental concerns have fared less well. On the positive side, there have been competitive elections between parties with strikingly different platforms. The media, in general, have begun to operate in a free and responsible manner, and the state security forces have largely been dismantled in most countries but not all. Can these forces reemerge? Yes, all too easily. On the negative side, politics in Central Europe, in a very real sense, was frozen in 1947-48. When the great thaw occurred more than forty years later, many of the ideas that reemerged were the conventional wisdom of that earlier period. As a result, divisive, bigoted, inflammatory views regarding race, ethnic origin, and religion remain. There has been a predictable rise in certain forms of intolerance:

- Neo-Nazis appeared in East Germany.
- Anti-Semitism rose again in Poland.
- The orchestrated goon squads again went on the rampage in Romania, and discrimination against the Hungarian minority population in Romania continued.
- Bulgaria continued its harsh treatment of ethnic Turks, and other minorities were suffering.

Most disturbing, however is the trend toward national disintegration. Greater Yugoslavia has fallen apart before our very eyes as centuries-old ethnic rivalries have taken on a decidedly lethal flavor. Similar ethnic tensions are on the rise elsewhere in Central Europe. The Slovak separatist movement triggered its counterpart among the Czechs, leading to the disintegration of a federal Czechoslovakia that had endured with considerable accomplishments during three-quarters of a century.

So the situation is mixed. We see great positive changes, but also great dangers and many potential pitfalls ahead.

The West, which had armed itself for four decades against the possibility of war with the Soviet Union and its Warsaw Pact allies, is in the interesting position of watching former adversaries become fast friends. In 1991, the Warsaw Pact died a quiet death, buried in the back pages of the *New York Times*. In its place the U. S. now sees like minded colleagues and potential trading partners. Clearly, this evolution is in the U. S. interest. The question is, what can the United States do and what are we doing to sustain the partial change which has occurred?

Foreign aid does not enjoy overwhelmingly popular support among the American people. Particularly at a time when the United States is suffering severe deficits and a general economic slowdown, there sometimes appears to be no constituency for increasing foreign aid. This is the case despite the fact that Secretary of Defense Richard Cheney outlined a program to reduce actual defense spending by over 25 percent during the early I990s. The Clinton administration intends even greater reductions. In part, this is a result of the changes in Europe, the so-called peace dividend. But this dividend is unlikely to be devoted to greater foreign assistance budgets. As a result, we must offer our assistance within the existing budgetary constraints. That is a simple fact.

Nonetheless, by diverting monies from other programs, and by extending existing programs to Eastern and Central Europe, the Congress and the administration were able to allocate some $320 million in bilateral assistance for the 1990 fiscal year and somewhat greater sums in subsequent years. A special appropriation was approved for Russia in 1992, but this will not affect East Central Europe directly. Former President Nixon recommended accelerated funding for Russia, President Clinton gave special attention to his views, but it was not clear whether the Congress would agree.

Given the domestic demand for resources, it is politically prudent for the United States to be very careful to make our assistance felt where it is needed most. And the United States must look for creative ways to assist the democratic process. There is a surprising degree of general agreement that the first priority of U. S. assistance must be private sector development. Successfully accomplishing the transition to a market economy is the single most important change that will improve the lives of those living in the region. Most of our assistance is, therefore, going into country-specific Enterprise Funds that the United States hopes will be able to stimulate private enterprise for years to come. And, as Most Favored Nation (MFN) status, U. S. Export-Import Bank eligibility, and Overseas Private Investment Corporation (OPIC) insurance guarantees are extended, American business relationships with private entities in Eastern Europe should grow at least moderately.

We have also approved a range of technical assistance. The Agency for International Development, the Treasury Department, the Environmental Protection Agency, the Labor Department, the Department of Defense, the Peace Corps, and other agencies are providing various forms of specialized expertise.

U. S. Assistance in Building Democracy

In the human rights area the U. S. has sought to assist the development of democratic institutions. The United States has been working to ensure that the people of Central Europe have a stake in the emerging democracies. The United States has been involved in a range of institution-building initiatives, but let me mention just a few.

Political Parties and Elections

The United States has made the decision to work with political parties, both at the national and grass-roots level, in hopes of giving the people the means of asserting a range of political choices. For example, countries in which the Communist party has fared well in their first electoral experience nations like Romania, Bulgaria, and Albania were those in which democratic parties were unwilling or incapable of organizing. This is not to suggest that the American electoral experience should be a universal model, but there was, and still is, a crying need for organization. Yet, the matter is somewhat delicate. As an outsider, the United States must not be seen as taking sides and supporting one party over another. To use a far-fetched example, if one can imagine that the will of the Czechoslovakian people had been to elect the Beer-drinker's party, the United States would have been wrong to undermine that effort. Assistance to political parties needs to be balanced and to reach a range of viable parties that are committed to democracy.

In Czechoslovakia, for example, the United States worked with political parties such as Civic Forum; the Slovakian party, Public against Violence; the Christian Democrats; and several other small parties. Assistance can be as basic as supplying telephones, typewriters, mimeograph machines, and paper. These materials are essential to any political organization, but are very expensive or in short supply in many places. The assistance has also been directed at the grass-roots level, with U. S. programs focused beyond the national capitals in provincial towns and villages.

One example was relayed to me by an American from the National Endowment for Democracy, who was assigned to work with Civic Forum candidates in the 1990 election. The candidates he worked with had lofty ideas. These candidates would go into the villages sounding like university professors, when the villagers were interested in the price of bread. American experts tried to respond to questions like: How do you take an opinion poll that yields meaningful information? How do you prepare a political commercial for television? How do parties convey their platform to the people? How do you sustain the party faithful after the first glow of electoral freedom has worn off? These are fairly simple questions, but in nations that have been denied free and fair elections the answers are not at all apparent.

In addition, the United States provided technical assistance throughout much of Central Europe to help ensure that elections would be fair. Take the ballot process. Since the outcome of communist elections was always a foregone conclusion, there was never any fear that the ballot box would be stuffed. With real candidates and real competition, however, the risk of election fraud becomes a serious concern. So Central Europeans have to begin thinking in terms of ballot paper that cannot be reproduced, indelible ink, tamper-proof ballot boxes, photo-ID badges, election observers, as well as the establishment of electoral tribunals.

The people of Central Europe clearly wanted free and fair elections, but translating that desire into reality required enormous planning and an on the job education in the electoral process. While the overwhelming success of the first round of elections was primarily a tribute to the people of the region, Americans and West Europeans can be pleased that they had a small but critical hand in facilitating that process.

Parliamentary Development

Strong legislatures are the most certain guarantees that the nations of Central Europe will never again fall victim to dictatorship. It is, therefore, not surprising that members of Congress like myself have been particularly sensitive to the need to develop strong and viable parliamentary institutions. There has been a dynamic outreach program to ensure that the parliamentary experiment succeeds.

The U. S. Information Agency has sponsored numerous parliamentary exchanges. For example, a group of six Czech and Slovak parliamentarians visited for a morning in my congressional office in Washington, discussing matters such as newsletters, constituent mail, and the role of my district office. These parliamentarians were particularly interested in talking with my press secretary about media relations. It is clear that an independent press, which may be favorable on some issues but unfavorable on others, was a new and unfamiliar phenomenon for these European parliamentarians.

That visit was by no means extraordinary. I had dinner with a group from the defense and intelligence oversight committee of the Czech and Slovak Parliament. They were in the United States to get some sense of how the U. S. Congress controls its armed forces and its intelligence forces. They were meeting with a wide range of people, from former Defense Secretary Dick Cheney and Chief of Staff General Colin Powell on down. Their questions were basic: How do you conduct investigations? What is involved in intelligence oversight? What happens if the defense ministry or the security forces lie to you? What happens when a military weapons system is canceled?

Just as the Central European parliamentarians are coming to the United States, so too are former U. S. members of Congress being enlisted or volunteered to offer technical advice in Prague, Warsaw, Budapest, and elsewhere. There they are tackling such issues as creating an effective parliamentary committee system and developing the expertise to ensure that legislatures do not become a rubber stamp for the various ministries. Such visits have the potential for great payoffs. These exchanges give parliamentarians a sense of what is possible.

As a final element of this parliament-building package, the United States is helping in the creation of law libraries for the national legislatures. While this may sound relatively inconsequential, it is, in fact, quite important. The new parliaments are in the process of drafting constitutions and totally revising their legal codes. Yet they do not have access to the wealth of material available. In many cases, they may lack the core documents, both from international law and their own historical national law, necessary to do their jobs. The United States and Western European nations are attempting to rectify this situation as quickly as possible.

Trade Union Assistance

The Communist leaders touted Central Europe as a worker's paradise, yet the common working person was oppressed in so many ways. There are heavy industries in Moravia and Silesia where the life span of the average worker has been shortened by ten years or more. Under the old regime, concern for workers' rights was nonexistent, common sense health and safety precautions were ignored, and official trade unions acted as the mouthpiece of the government. Moreover, as the regional economies make the transition to a free market, entirely new relationships must be established between labor and management.

It is not surprising, therefore, that the U. S. democracy-building initiatives should seek to establish viable trade unions that can reflect worker concerns. The goal is to assist labor unions throughout the region to develop in the way that Solidarity has developed in Poland. The United States has provided communications and printing equipment, outreach and educational programs, and organizational assistance throughout Central Europe.

Lessons Learned Regarding Democratization Assistance

These, then, are the sorts of democratization projects that the United States is undertaking. Many Western Europeans, notably Germans, are also deeply involved in rendering such assistance. Some of our efforts have been wonderfully successful, others decidedly less so.

Are there any lessons that can be drawn from Western experience thus far?

First, it would be dangerous to assume that, just because political and human rights breakthroughs have been achieved, the West can dispense with the task of democracy building. The fighting in former Yugoslavia is a grim testament to the dangers faced in the state-building process. Given the potential for demagoguery, it is necessary to support the entire range of democratic institutions the legislature, academia, trade unions, media, and business.

Second, the West needs to be constantly reminded of the remarkable nature of the changes in Central Europe. Obstacles to successful democratic reform are numerous and formidable. Nations must quite literally rewrite nearly every law. Accordingly, ground-breaking new legislation is being enacted virtually every week in countries like Hungary and Poland. The United States needs to be understanding of and prepare for the inevitable fits and starts that the democratic process undergoes. We in the West must not be disappointed when, on occasion, events do not surpass our wildest dreams. There will be disillusionment too, for expectations are very high and economic conditions inevitably deteriorate before they improve.

Third, as the process unfolds, the West must support the process of political reform and not be aligned with any particular participant in the process. There have been a few giants who stood out Walesa in Poland, Havel in the former Czechoslovakia, and Yeltsin in Russia. Certainly the West must do all it can to assist these popularly elected leaders as they pursue market-orientated policies, pluralism, and democratization. But we should recognize that there comes a time when Czechoslovakia is not led by Vaclav Havel or even when there is no Czechoslovakia. There will be a time when the Polish people do not rely on Lech Walesa for guidance or at least inspiration. It is therefore the process that we must focus upon and support, not the person. We must help develop democratic institutions rather than focus on personalities.

Fourth, as the process of democratization proceeds, it is important to utilize all available forms of assistance. This chapter has only referred to the U. S. effort, but the European Community (EC) has similar programs. In addition, the Commission on Security and Cooperation in Europe (CSCE), which has long been involved in human rights in Europe, has great potential to contribute to the advancement of democracy.

Lastly, the United States and other Western states should recognize the limits of their ability to influence the course of events in Central Europe. The concepts of democracy and freedom carry enormous power, and the fact that the very diverse nations of most Eastern states are able to embrace freedom should offer promise for the future of Central Europe. The United States, as a democratic state, shares in a collective responsibility to assist in the transition. The United States, however, should never lose sight of the fact that the course and the pace of democratization in the eastern region of the new Europe is ultimately the decision of the people themselves.

6

Theoretical and Psychological Approaches for Human Rights

Introduction

The inquiries are distinct but not separate because punishment of offenders may itself be a form of redress for victims, whereas measures like truth telling, aimed at redress, may have punitive aspects.

The Relevance of Theories of Punishment

Criminal justice theorists generally divide punishment rationales into two broad categories utilitarian and retributive. Utilitarians "believe that the right act is that which produces the greatest utility, or is most conducive to the welfare of all those affected by the act." Punishment, in the utilitarian's mind, is future oriented and consequential, focusing specifically on end results. If punishment prevents an act that society has designated as a "wrong," it is justified. Utilitarians are not concerned with the amount or character of the offender's culpability. After determining which rights and privileges to protect, a utilitarian society uses punishment to "persuade" people to respect those rights.

A theory based on end results alone lends itself to potential abuse. For example, society could use torture to deter crime. Utilitarians counter accusations of moral abuse by integrating into their theory a balancing of the costs of curtailing certain citizens' civil rights against the benefits of punishment. The harm to the individual offender cannot outweigh the benefit of the punishment to society. If it does, the punishment is not justifiable.

Utilitarian punishment may be based on deterrence, rehabilitation, or incapacitation or on some combination of these.

Deterrence

Deterrence justifies punishment because it functions as a social control, using persuasion, propaganda, fear, and other forms of social coercion to prevent crime. Intuitively deterrence works because "the risk of unpleasant consequences is a very strong motivational factor for most people in most situations." Utilitarians assume that people assess their actions rationally in light of the possibility they will be caught and punished, and this assumption is the core of a deterrence model. The greater the likelihood of punishment, the more likely people are to refrain from committing crimes.

Deterrence may be special or general. Special deterrence targets the individual "not the crime but the criminal to be punished." The utilitarian assumes that an individual will not commit a crime because prior experiences provide incentives to avoid repetition. General deterrence targets society as a whole it is the ability of criminal law and its enforcement to make citizens law abiding, either through the law's moral authority or through habit, social imitation, fear, and coercion.

Deterrence theory provides several problems when applied to state-sponsored or initiated crimes in the human rights context. To deter, the content of the protected norm must be clear to both the enforcing entity and the potential offender. In cases of state violation of human rights, potential abusers may not always perceive that their act violates a norm. Often their confusion results from society's mixed messages: National security or the need to restore order, for example, may be invoked to justify what would otherwise be clearly punishable acts such as torture or murder. Because government and society may justify or condone certain abuses, human rights abusers may not see their acts as ones that need to be deterred.

A second difficulty arises when individual members of organizations that abuse basic human rights ignore special deterrence factors because their organizational façade protects them. In the military, for example, immediate and certain approval from comrades overrides any reason for complying with legal standards or any fear of the consequences of engaging in criminal behavior. The certainty of approval and support from comrades and superior officers neutralizes the deterrent effect of a possible criminal sanction. Approval or disapproval from the military environment is much stronger than rejection from society at large.

Similar results may occur within monolithic political party structures. These effects may be particularly pronounced at lower levels of the command structure, where autonomy is most reduced and the pull of institutional approval is greatest. Because individual offenders do not believe the threat of punishment, deterrence in these situations becomes an empty shell. Moreover, past experience with de facto ordejure impunity may confirm to members of such organizations that they have little to fear from criminal sanctions. Therefore, for a deterrent threat to be credible, enforcement may have to come from outside the country in which the abuses occurred.

Rehabilitation and Incapacitation

Rehabilitation focuses on the offender's reeducation and his or her reintegration into society. Besides reeducating the offender, rehabilitation has two other potential results: (1) the offender may attain some semblance of a "meaningful" life, and (2) society can restrain the offender using social controls.

Rehabilitation assumes that the offender is capable of absorbing and retaining social norms through education and rejects the possibility that an offender might resist reform. Originally, criminologists interested in punishment believed that scientific advances would facilitate rehabilitation. In recent years, however, theorists have begun to doubt the efficacy of a rehabilitation model because recidivism appears to occur at the same rate in programs that focus on rehabilitation as in those programs that do not.

Rehabilitation poses several difficulties in the context of state-sponsored or condoned criminal violations. It assumes society has both the right and the obligation to rehabilitate an offender by changing his attitudes and perspectives. Yet here these attitudes are neither personal nor aberrational rather, they are deliberately inculcated in an institutional setting, as part of a larger mission, say, of national security, that may still be seen as valid. Rehabilitation in this context means institutional reformation. Although such rehabilitation is no doubt a worthy and necessary enterprise, it requires time, money, and political will and is a different enterprise than changing individual offenders. A similar objection applies to a theory based on incapacitation, which merely seeks to remove the offender from society's midst.

Retribution

In contrast to the utilitarians, adherents of retributive theories look backward to the nature of the offender's act and to his or her culpability. The wrongdoer deserves a punishment proportionate to his or her culpability.

Retribution is based on moral culpability. "If the criminal deserves punishment, it should be inflicted. If the criminal is not morally culpable, however, no punishment is justified, regardless of any potential good effect it may have on society." Moreover, retribution is sometimes justified as a substitute for revenge a socially acceptable way of avoiding blood feuds or vendettas while allowing society to express its deeply held moral revulsion at the criminal act. Other theorists explain the retributive urge as an expression of deeply held human sentiments of rage against behavior we see as oppressive or violative of our self-respect: Those sentiments are channeled through social institutions rather than allowed to fester.

The retributivist model links punishment to the offender's failure to accept and adopt generally accepted moral, social, or legal standards. Retribution is based upon an offender's understanding of his or her crime. The enforcer normally attempts to achieve justice by focusing either on the offender's moral reprehensiveness or on the offender's "unjust enrichment" through a voluntary rejection of the burdens of living within society's rules.

Theorists who focus on the reprehensiveness of offenders reject a strict separation between the moral and the legal, understanding the latter as a laudable and necessary attempt to give form to sentiments of resentment arising from the offender's denial of our self-worth. Under an "unjust enrichment" model, society institutes rules and laws to govern social interaction. To guarantee peace among citizens, social rules burden each citizen by limiting his or her freedom to choose certain actions. Thus, the person who commits a crime is not sharing fully in the responsibilities and burdens of citizenship. The enforcer, usually government, punishes the offender to restore balance. This approach assumes the offender receives some benefit from breaking the rules. In the context of state sponsored crimes, individuals who participated in a repressive enterprise received job security, status, and a psychological sense of superiority at times, as in Eastern Europe, material gain was indeed part of the bargain. On the other hand, in some cases the perpetrator may well not be pursuing any personal gain but merely doing his job; if so, an offender-based retributivist justification loses much of its force.

Besides focusing on culpability, retributivists measure the proportionality of punishment. In its purest form, retribution took the form of lex talionis, or an "eye for an eye, a tooth for a tooth, a life for a life." Current retributive models differ slightly. In them, the central organizing principle of sentencing is that of "commensurate desserts." Sentences are to be proportionate in their severity to the gravity of the defendant's criminal conduct. Thus, retributivism aims to restore balance to society.

Denunciation Model of Punishment

Both utilitarian and retributivist accounts of punishment have been widely criticized as limited by their own opposing premises: Retributivism requires the infliction of pain on offenders even if doing so cannot be shown to serve any future social good, whereas utilitarian accounts have difficulty coming to terms with the moral imperative of punishing only those who are guilty and doing so in proportion to the moral quality of the offense. Two alternative theories that attempt to combine and improve on the strengths of each approach hold more promise as the moral and theoretical underpinnings of a theory of punishment for state-sponsored or condoned human rights violations. A denunciation model of punishment focuses on the symbolic and norm-creating qualities of punishment for the larger society, whereas "goal-oriented retributivism" emphasizes the effects of punishment on the victim of crime. To the extent it is victim centered, this theory views punishment itself as a form of redress.

In the past, societies traditionally used punishment "as an opportunity for symbolic expression of moral outrage against non-conformity." Modern accounts of denunciation theory see punishment as an expression of moral criticism. As such, it aims, first, at bringing wrongdoers to acknowledge their misdeeds and change their behavior and, second, at providing moral guidance more generally. The model is both backward looking, in that moral criticism is based on an offender's past acts, and forward looking, in that its goal is to change future behavior by establishing clear societal standards against which such behavior may be measured. In addition, in its broadest expression denunciation theory focuses not only on the offender but on the "satisfaction" of the law-abiding members of a society. Whereas a utilitarian focuses on deterrence as a way of increasing safety, a denunciation theorist emphasizes the need to increase societal satisfaction with a just scheme of punishment, thus increasing social cohesion. Law in this model serves as a forum for ordered, fair resolution of disputes that threaten the social fabric, but also, more subtly, by (a) announcing the norms of the community and thus reifying the values embedded in the culture and (b) establishing structures that create or sustain social behavior consistent with those values.

A denunciation-type theory seems particularly appropriate in cases of state sponsored or condoned human rights violations. The state, after all, plays a large role in articulating the moral values to be enshrined in laws: If those values become debased through state abuses and human rights violations, the state should play a major role in reformulating them for society. In addition, denunciation may sufficiently shame past perpetrators of abuse that they do not commit similar atrocities. Neither individuals nor regimes gladly accept the label torturer or murderer. For a denunciation theory to be effective, punishment must be public and must clearly enunciate standards of behavior. It must also be severe enough to make the intended point a mere slap on the wrist might otherwise lead to the conclusion that the norms of the community do not, in fact, find the behavior at issue reprehensible at all.

Whereas denunciation theories of punishment focus on the norm-creating and enforcing effect of punishment, what Jaime Malamud-Goti has called "goal-oriented" retributivism focuses on the effect of punishment on the victim of the offense. Both utilitarianism and retribution classically acknowledge the victim of an offense only peripherally, to the extent needed to punish the offender or establish the greater good. Retribution, in its purest form, is offender centered, and all offenses that lie at parallel moral levels should receive equivalent amounts of punishment. When the victim is the center of the punishment equation, however, vindication becomes important, and similar offenses may be resolved in an entirely distinct manner. One victim might be satisfied with a symbolic demonstration of the state's willingness to acknowledge the victim's trauma whereas another victim might require more. Similarly, such a theory would not be able to override the victims' needs by subordinating them to a calculus of greatest overall societal good.

Punishment and Redress

The idea that wrongs should be redressed, that reparation should be made to the injured, is among the most venerable and most central of legal principles. It was a major proposition of the natural law dating from the time of Moses through Grotius and St. Thomas Aquinas; indeed, one interpretation of the lex talionis is that it refers to the need for restitution (an eye for an eye), not merely retribution. The Prophet Muhammad admonished that if you see a wrong you must redress it, with your hand [action] if you can, otherwise with your tongue [vocal condemnation], otherwise with your eyes [reprobation], otherwise in your heart and that is the weakest manifestation of your faith [conviction].

All modern societies allow for some form of civil redress for harm to individuals, and most contain administrative procedures for redress when the harm is occasioned by agents of the state as well as special forms of redress when the harm comes about as a result of a criminal act.

A victim-centered view of punishment blurs the line between criminal punishment and civil redress, seeing the criminal sanction as a form of redress and civil penalties as having punitive value. The distinction between civil and criminal penalties is based on the view that criminal acts transcend the harm to any one individual, harming the entire society and requiring punitive action by the state; in contrast, civil wrongs concern the victim alone. The distinction was almost unknown in ancient law: Under the Code of Hammurabi, the death-fine of ancient Greece, the Law of Moses, the restitution required by Indian Hinduism, and the early German "redemption of revenge," compensation to the victim was considered an integral part of the sanction for crime.

The tort-crime distinction is usually traced back to twelfth-century England, when feudal barons decided to increase their revenues by obtaining fines and forfeitures from offenders at the expense of victims. While well entrenched in nineteenth- and early twentieth-century Anglo-American legal practice, this distinction was never unanimously accepted by scholars. In Continental practice (and in the countries of Latin America, Africa, and Asia that imported the precepts of the Napoleonic Code), the distinction was never as clear cut. In France, for example, an injured party may file an *action civile* for civil damages in criminal court concurrently with the criminal case or *action publique*, acting as a kind of private prosecutor; this practice avoids the delay and expense to the crime victim of using the civil courts. In a number of countries, the public prosecutor may represent the victim in the civil case as well as prosecute the criminal action.

Even in common law countries, recent years have seen renewed interest in the plight and role of the crime victim. Most courts now provide for court-ordered restitution. Redress for victims is justified to prevent the alienation of victims from society and to encourage voluntary citizen participation in crime reporting, as added deterrence for criminals, and to prevent individuals from refraining from revenge or self-help in the wake of victimization. Victims are encouraged to participate in sentencing decisions, and their testimony is heard in deciding whether aggravating circumstances exist in capital cases. Conversely, civil sanctions like forfeiture of property are increasingly recognized as having a punitive result, thus requiring elaborate due process safeguards.

Content of a Victim-Centered Approach

A victim-centered approach to punishment, as well as questions of redress for victims more generally, requires an analysis of victims' needs in the wake of state initiated or sponsored crime against the victim or the victim's immediate family. To some extent, psychological studies of victimization are helpful in evaluating these needs.

Psychologists have long noted the traumatic effects of victimization. Because violent crimes like those at issue here lay bare the fragility of life and the possibility of death, they deprive victims not only of "their belief in invulnerability, but also of [their] sense of control and autonomy in the world." In response, victims may sink into helplessness and experience a loss of control over their destiny. Victimization also can lead to increased isolation because the world becomes a more frightening and less explicable place. In a human rights context, this isolation may be particularly keen for victims and their family members, who may be shunned by the larger society as political outcasts who brought their problems on themselves, or from a generalized fear of being tainted or even found guilty by association with the victim. Survivors of traumatic experiences also feel isolated because others cannot bear to hear about and be linked with the massive pain of the experience and so tend to shun anyone they associate with it.

In providing redress for victims, therefore, it is important to find ways to reassert their sense of control and autonomy, lessen their isolation, and increase their feeling of belonging to a community. Another important insight from the psychological literature is the need for victims to find some meaning in their victimization. Whereas when the victim was a clearly defined and active political opponent of the regime the reason for victimization may be clear, in many cases victims of the most egregious human rights violations have no idea why they were victimized. The families may be similarly baffled.

Studies of torture victims in Chile, for instance, showed that production of a written document systematizing and summarizing their experiences was therapeutic because it helped the victims "integrate the traumatic experience into their lives by identifying its significance in the context of political and social events as well as the context of their personal history." In addition, producing testimony about the traumatic events helped channel the victim's anger into a socially constructive action and provided a form of catharsis. Psychologists found that the power of the testimonies derived in part from the autoassertive quality of simple verbalization of the experience.

A conclusion to be drawn from the psychological literature on victimization, then, is that a victim-centered approach to redress must provide victims with a sense of control, an ability to lessen their isolation and be reintegrated into their community, and the possibility of finding reintegration and meaning through participation in the process. But what kind of process will lead to these results?

One aspect of the answer deals with the modalities of redress: These should focus on enhancing the dignity of the victims and on public recognition of the wrong done them as much as on monetary compensation or provision of public services. Redress may include public apologies and atonement by representatives of the state, monetary and non monetary compensation, preferential access to public services or resources, reinstatement or rehabilitation, disclosure of the truth, and commemoration, as well as punishment for those responsible for the victimization. In all these areas, the touchstone of redress is its effect on the victim.

To the extent redress works through legal measures, some insights into what effective redress entails may come from work on procedural justice done in the context of civil and criminal litigation in the United States. Procedural justice theorists start from the premise that people are sensitive to the process and procedures they experience in encounters with the law. They posit that the fairness with which an individual is treated in encounters with the legal system, more than the outcome, is the most important factor in determining that person's perception of justice. People value the opportunity to state their views to a decision maker regardless of the influence of those views on the outcome of a dispute. The dignity accorded the person within the procedure, the symbolic features of the procedure, and the degree of control the person has over the procedure (rather than the outcome) are all perceived components of fairness. These value-expressive effects reinforce citizens' positive self-image and standing in a social group. These findings are consonant with the need to reestablish autonomy and dignity, as discussed earlier.

Several studies address specifically the kinds of procedures most likely to promote a perception of procedural fairness. One early influential study compared the highly formalized procedures of adversarial litigation with less formal, less adversarial forms of mediation aimed at a prelitigation settlement. The study compared litigants' perceptions of fairness after trial and after negotiated settlement of a dispute. It found that, irrespective of whether they had won or lost, litigants viewed adversarial proceedings like trial and binding arbitration as fairer and more satisfactory than negotiated settlement. The most important explanations of this preference were that the trial-type proceedings were seen as more dignified and more careful. A formal court hearing was perceived as according importance to the persons and subject matter involved in a dispute, whereas an informal settlement conference might have seemed to trivialize the issue of right and wrong that litigants perceived was at the heart of their claim. In addition, formal trial procedures were seen as offering more participation in decision making than informal means and as being more understandable.

Subsequent studies have attempted to control for cultural specificity in the preference for one type of procedure over another. While researchers found, for example, that Chinese subjects were more likely than U.S. subjects to prefer mediation over a full adversarial hearing, they found that both subject groups use the same criteria for decision making: control over presentation of evidence, the fairness of the procedure, the capacity of the procedure to reduce animosity between the disputants, and the extent to which the procedure favored the subject. Other studies have reaffirmed the preference for adversary-type procedures and have isolated the ability to define the issues under dispute, to express arguments and present evidence, and to cross-examine or seek clarification as essential components of disputants' preference for such procedures. Finally, new studies show that adversary type procedures are especially preferred when the relationship between the parties is such that negotiation and trade-offs are not possible as in the relationship between victims and victimizers in human rights cases.

Although it is important not to draw too much from these studies or to minimize the differences between U.S. legal culture and that of other countries, the conclusions do suggest several things. First, any victim-centered procedure must put a heavy emphasis on people being able to tell their story fully before a decision maker who is perceived as neutral, honest, and attentive. Respectful treatment is more important than monetary or other gain. Public airing of victims' stories seems to serve important psychological and therapeutic ends. This finding again points up the usefulness of public recognition of the wrong done, public apologies, monuments, commemorations, reburials, and other forms of symbolic redress as important methods in a victim-centered approach. It further suggests that compensation alone is insufficient; indeed, compensation may be counterproductive if it infringes on victims' dignity through, for instance, excessive or too searching application procedures. The same is true of compensation that is seen as buying silence or "blood money." The finding also suggests that states may have some flexibility in meeting the needs of victims: Incarceration of offenders may not be the only option.

Second, more formalized procedures, including the ability to have an advocate and to confront and question their victimizers, may be more satisfying for victims than less formal, less adjudicative models. This finding might suggest the superiority of trial-type procedures, either civil or as an adjunct to criminal process, as preferable to more legislative or commission-type procedures from the point of view of victims.

Further confirmation of this last point comes from the experiences of Holocaust survivors. Although a number of techniques history books, films, classes, and the like are important to maintaining memory and teaching history, only trials, by bringing the past into the present and giving it present effects, satisfied the victims' need for justice. As

Henry Rousso wrote of the 1983 trial of Klaus Barbie in France:

> *Teaching history and raising consciousness are praiseworthy goals, but other institutions could achieve them as well as the courts. Nothing but a trial could satisfy the victims' need for justice, however. And their statements after the trial made it clear that this was what they felt too, far more than they cared about participating in any educational process.*

This kind of victim-centered model using modalities of redress combines easily with the utilitarian model as well as with a victim-centered retributive model of punishment. Public scorn for both the practices employed and those who employed them serves as a powerful deterrent. Publication of the names of those found to have committed murders, inflicted torture, and caused disappearances, although not a penal sanction, serves as a kind of punishment. For that very reason, some countries and commentators have hesitated to release names without a full judicial process.

Clemency and Punishment

Historically a "living fossil, a relic from the days when an all-powerful monarch possessed the power to punish and to remit punishment as an act of mercy," the power of clemency exists in almost all legal systems. Clemency may take a number of different forms, including pardon, amnesty, commutation of sentence, or remission of fines. For purposes of this book, there are two salient differences: First, pardon or commutation is granted to individuals on the basis of individualized considerations, whereas amnesty is granted to groups on the basis of public policy concerns. Second, pardon generally does not vitiate guilt for the underlying offense, whereas amnesty operates as an extinction of the offense itself.

Both utilitarian and retributivist theories limit the use of clemency. General deterrence requires certainty of punishment: If potential lawbreakers are not convinced of this certainty, they will be encouraged to commit crimes. Although the rules themselves may be humane and may try to avoid unnecessary suffering, they must make no exceptions. Thus, Jeremy Bentham decried the extensive use of pardons in the late eighteenth century because they undermined the certainty of sanctions:

> From pardon power unrestricted, comes impunity to delinquency in all shapes: from impunity to delinquency in all shapes, impunity to maleficence in all shapes: from impunity to maleficence in all shapes, dissolution of government: from dissolution of government, dissolution of political society.

For utilitarians, therefore, any exceptions to punishment must be carefully and narrowly drawn if used at all.

Early retributivists, like early utilitarians, believed that punishment was a "categorical imperative"; for Immanuel Kant, failure of a society to punish those who deserved punishment would make the members of that society themselves guilty of injustice. This was so because punishment was required to right a balance, to take away an injust benefit to the criminal. Pardons by a sovereign were in most cases unwarranted because they took away the citizen's right to have the balance of societal burdens and benefits restored. Even for Kant, however, pardon or remission of punishment was acceptable when the crime was encouraged by the state whose laws forbid it, as, for instance, those convicted of dueling. Arguably, grave human rights violations committed by individuals in the employ of the state fall into a similar category.

Modern theorists have tried to develop a principled set of rules to distinguish appropriate uses of the power of clemency from those that erode justice. Kathleen Moore sums up the bounds of clemency compatible with justice as those where (1) the offender is legally or morally innocent, (2) the offender gained no unfair advantage by the crime, (3) the action was either morally justified or at least "conscientious," or (4) the offender would suffer excessively. Reasons (1) and (4) seem the easiest to justify. Surely an appropriate use of the clemency power is to right individual cases of miscarriage of justice or of overly severe sentencing: to allow greater individuation in how we treat each offender given uniform sentencing laws and fallible truth finding. The closest analogue in the human rights context is probably mitigation of punishment in cases of obedience to superior orders.

So too with mercy based on the individual's frailties or personal tragedies: the dismissal of cases of those offenders too old or too infirm to be worth trying and punishing. On the other hand, the category of moral justification seems most slippery; who is to decide when a prohibited action is morally justified? No doubt the military establishments of Latin America believe their actions during the 1970s were morally justified in the name of saving the country from Communist expansion. Is that enough? I believe not.

Beyond these, several religious traditions encompass ideas of mercy and forgiveness that might form an independent moral basis for clemency. However, even within these traditions, forgiveness is possible only on the basis of an "offer of compensation" that is, the recognition of wrongs committed and atonement through acts of reparation. Although scholars disagree on whether mercy not tied to justice has a place in the law, even those who admit some independent role for mercy see it as a waiver of the right to punish that can be exercised only (either actually or by some process of agency) by those who have been victimized.

Summary

The theories of punishment that best apply in the case of state-sponsored or condoned human rights violations are those which focus on the effects of punishment on the victim and on the wider society. Both denunciation theory and victim-centered retribution require punishment as one of an array of measures designed to provide redress for victims and to establish the force of societal norms. The following chapters illustrate how international law treats the concepts of punishment and redress as necessary parts of a legal regime based on respect for human rights.

7

Human Rights in the Europe

Introduction

Many students of human rights would settle for satisfactory explanations as to why attention to a range of human rights rose and fell within one state over time, much less why attention to rights varies by state. When taking European states as a whole, it is so difficult to summarize factors and trends that reasonable persons can disagree on whether there is a new Europe or not. It is true that there were so many human rights problems that the so-called new Europe sometimes looked very similar to the old Europe prior to 1989 or even prior to 1945.

Nevertheless, we are faced with the legitimate question of the fate of universal human rights in that part of Europe dominated by communists for forty to seventy years. To paraphrase Jack Donnelly in this volume, one can move from one type of brutal authoritarianism to another. Or one can move from authoritarianism to a more liberal regime in which at least the extent of human rights violations is reduced. Or one can move to a democracy, characterized minimally by reasonably free and fair elections, although that does not guarantee that any specified portion of universal human rights will be respected. Any number of genuinely elected governments have violated any number of universal human rights; they continue to do so. Or, finally, one can move to a rights-protective regime. When we look at the old Soviet bloc, where do we see progress towards a rights protective regime, and where do we see major problems? And, what accounts for these problems and areas of progress?

National Factors

There is little reason to doubt the conventional wisdom that the key to rights behavior is found mostly within a state. The political attitudes of a people or peoples associated with a state is the primary key, most of the time, to the practice of rights. But this conventional wisdom unfortunately leads us into a murky area.

Neither political scientists dealing with the concept "political culture," nor historians dealing with the concept "national character" have been able to provide either convincing explanations of the past or sound predictions about the future. Part of the problem is that within one nation, much less within a binational or multinational state, there can be more than one political culture meaning a set of attitudes toward government and public policy. One such set of attitudes may be dominant for a time but that can change. Some comparativists in political science have given up on using "political culture" as an explanatory variable, believing that studies to date have not yielded sufficiently clear results. And no wonder.

Historians and political scientists told us for some time that especially Russia but also the Soviet Union had an authoritarian and deferential political culture not sympathetic to democracy or a broader range of human rights. But in August 1991, tens of thousands in Moscow and Leningrad took to the streets in support of democracy, human rights, and Boris Yeltsin, and in opposition to authoritarian communism. We are, of course, speaking of a few thousand persons out of a Soviet population of over 250 million. Nevertheless, there was a crucial degree of assertive public support for at least more civil and political rights in a supposedly deferential political culture. As the well-known Soviet scholar and former diplomat, George Kennan, said on television shortly thereafter, there had never been anything like that show of public support for human rights in all of Russia's history. So, in supposedly authoritarian and deferential Russia, by 1991 we found the Soviet Congress adopting a declaration on human rights that said in its first article: "Every person possesses natural, inalienable and inviolable rights and freedoms. They are sealed in laws that must correspond to the universal declaration of human rights, the international covenants on human rights and other international norms."

While not doubting the key factor of a people's attitude toward government and public policy for the stable practice of human rights, one trying to derive systematic propositions on this subject on a global basis finds more perplexity than clarity. For example, with regard to civil and political rights, some nations have shown an affinity for the practice of democratic rights over a fair amount of time, only to find themselves in an authoritarian system. The relatively recent examples of Uruguay and Chile come immediately to mind.

In the other direction, we think we know that democratic occupation, education, and legal engineering helped transform authoritarian Germany and Japan into rights-protective regimes. In both cases, however, the previous authoritarian regime had been completely discredited. What do we know about more peaceful, less abrupt transformations not entailing foreign occupation and imposed restructuring?

Looking at Taiwan, for example, one might conclude that authoritarianism can give birth to a rights-protective regime, or something close to it, via economic growth combined with equitable distribution of benefits, a relatively large middle class, broad education, experience with perhaps local elections, and a nonviolent transfer of leadership. South Korea may be on a similar path. James Turner Johnson, however, would add, especially, the factor of civic organizations that mediate between the atomized individual and the domineering state. Other scholars stress still other factors as being necessary for a rights-protective regime to emerge.

There are not many areas of the old European communist world that combine encouraging factors. Moreover, in the examples of Taiwan and South Korea, rights practices emerged over half a century, not immediately after creation of the governing system. This East Asian analogy, if applicable to Eastern Europe and the former Soviet Union (which may be debated) would suggest that stable rights-protective national regimes will be arriving in many areas of the old communist Europe only after considerable time has elapsed, if ever.

In this volume, Donnelly and the editor stress national factors as primary in the practice of rights, but they do not offer us European specifics regarding this point. John Hibbing, Josef Blahož, Pavel Hollander, and Bruce Garver get into the specifics of political attitudes of peoples, but without indicating what does or does not produce a political culture supportive of democracy or extensive rights practice. Hibbing and Hollander note that many political attitudes extant in Eastern Europe give cause for alarm about, for Hibbing, legislative competence and stability, and for Hollander, attitudes in general in Slovakia.

Many observers believe that one of the greatest dangers in this part of the world is chauvinistic nationalism, in which the aggrandizement of a people supersedes all else. The Serbian example in the former greater Yugoslavia is perhaps the clearest case of this old problem, but another is the more peaceful form of the same phenomenon in Slovakia, also given attention by several authors here.

Violence in several parts of the former Soviet Union has its origin in the same tendency to violate the rights of others, including the right to life, in the name of the higher good, and especially of the power and independence, of a people. Sri Lanka, for a time one of the better examples among developing countries of commitment to a broad range of rights despite poverty, has come unglued primarily because of Sinhalese assertions of majority power and prosperity, which provoked a violent reaction by many Sri Lankan Tamils.

A very relevant question is whether a combination of human rights education and legal engineering can ameliorate the destructive appeal of chauvinistic ethnicity and nationalism, as well as other attitudes incompatible with the practice of human rights. Can legal engineering and human rights education produce the type of political culture supportive of a rights-protective regime? Hibbing, in particular, wants to see an end to constant legal tinkering on the part of East European states, so that one democratic constitution and one set of electoral and other provisions for public authority can have some impact on a state over time. Richard Claude shows clearly that East European states might well profit from looking at what the Philippines has done to institutionalize human rights education in a formal and non-formal way. Likewise, Vaclav Trojan shows what was tried by way of formal human rights education in Czechoslovakia between 1989 and 1992.

Of course, both legal engineering and education, whether formal, non-formal, or informal (as those terms are used by Claude), take time to have effect. In some cases it would seem that legal engineering produced some effects beneficial for the practice of human rights. One can think of Charles DeGaulle's Fifth French Republic and its different electoral laws and new double executive; democratic France under the rules of the Fifth has been more stable than under those of the Third or Fourth Republics. It seems something of a stroke of genius to have created two rounds of voting in

France. The French can engage in their apparent passion for protest voting on the first round, then be forced into a political consensus when the protest parties and candidates do not receive enough votes to be retained on the ballot in the second round. Political stability in democratic France has been enhanced by the electoral laws since 1958. A movement in Israel is growing to rewrite that country's electoral laws in quest of majority rule and decisive policies instead of coalition government and policy immobilism.

Moreover, it may be true that in many Western democracies there has been so much education for human rights in various forms that a radical departure from extensive civil and political rights has become "subrationally unthinkable." One would like to think that in most states in the North Atlantic area, for example, the probability of authoritarian government is nearly zero. Yet legal engineering and human rights education, when they occur in a socio-economic context unfriendly to rights practice, can only with difficulty lead to progress.

Moreover, we know from many empirical studies in states like the United States that even after over two hundred years of rights practice, many Americans do not hold attitudes compatible with international standards on civil and political rights, much less on economic and social rights. While some Americans despair that in contemporary times certain West European democratic provinces manifest a resurgence of racist and xenophobic sentiments reaching up to about 15% of the voters in local elections, some West Europeans despair that a former fascist and Klansman like David Duke in Louisiana could poll almost 45 percent of the vote for governor. Thus, it may be more crucial for a political elite to hold values supportive of human rights than for the masses to do so. Paradoxically, rights have been practiced in the democratic West despite intolerant and authoritarian views on the part of many citizens.

It is unfortunately true that while many hope for a beneficial effect on human rights from post-communist laws and education, in the short term, many problems confront post-communist European leaders in the I990s. We simply do not yet know whether the effort to construct governing and educational systems sympathetic to human rights can endure the problems of demagogic politicians, poor economic conditions, rampant nationalisms of various sorts, and the other pitfalls inherent in an attempted transformation from communist totalitarianism to rights-protective regimes.

It is impressive that states like Czechoslovakia (or at least the Czech lands), Hungary, Poland, and to a much lesser extent Bulgaria and Russia, have been led by persons committed to entrenching internationally recognized human rights in new national constitutions and statutes. One cannot read the sections by Blahož, Hollander, and Hibbing without being impressed with the attempt in East Central Europe, at least, to move toward democratic state capitalism. One does not have to believe that such a move constitutes an end to history to say that the values found in the International Bill of Rights (IBR), covering civil-political and socioeconomic rights, are similar to the early state-building efforts in these post-communist states. Note that we are not saying that the influence of the IBR per se has generated broad influence, but rather that the values found in these new state constitutions are fully compatible with, and explicitly linked to, the IBR. To put it a bit crudely for reasons of emphasis, that complex of human rights instruments calls for Sweden writ large, and that is what these eastern states are trying to construct.

Moreover, many of the former communist states in Europe have explicitly accepted international human rights treaties, as indicated in Annex H of this book. It was of more than passing interest that the Commonwealth of Independent States, in Article 2 of its basic document, affirmed that "each of the agreeing parties guarantees citizens of other parties and also people without citizenship who reside on its territory, regardless of nationality or other difference, civil, political, social, economic and cultural rights and freedoms in accordance with common international norms on human rights." In the national constitutions in Eastern Europe, there is no one model of governance and rights that emerges across the region. Blahož shows that with regard to the judiciary, some West European experiences affected constitutional developments in the CSFR, Hungary, and Poland. Yet overall, one cannot say that the U. S. model, or the British model, or any continental model has dominated eastern state building after 1989. This suggests that differing national factors will lead to a variety of schemes to implement the principles of democratic state-capitalism.

At the other end of the scale, it is also quite clear not only in the former Yugoslavia but also in Romania and Albania that progress in stable rights practice has been meagre. When one broadens the picture to include Georgia, Moldavia, Albania, and Azerbaijan, among other new eastern states, it is clear that the obstacles to a rights-protective regime are major.

There *are* different categories of states in terms of the prospects for adherence to international standards of human rights. In some cases it is clear enough that history was indeed frozen by communist leaders in the sense that historical animosities were not solved or even ameliorated during repressive control. And it is clear enough that there was precious little education for human rights, whether in areas dominated by Moscow or by other forms of authoritarianism, as in Romania and Yugoslavia. This paucity was so despite the fact that most of the European communist states were technically parties to many human rights treaties. But the evident lack of serious or good faith attention to human rights values, especially via education, should remind us not to overemphasize the importance of technical adherence to those treaties. When communist totalitarianism fell, old feuds from before World War II, or even World War I, resurfaced. That is why, for example, the Balkans in 1992 looked very much like it did in 1912 or

1914. And that is why certain peoples incorporated into the Russian and Soviet empires by force were violently seeking to redress grievances from a long time ago.

These areas, with layers of problems accumulated over the years, will find it extremely difficult to do more than liberalize that is, to do more than curtail some of the most repressive and exploitative features of Marxism-Leninism. Some of these states may not progress much beyond the situation found in the old Soviet Union under Gorbachev : the absolute terror of the Stalin period was curtailed, but the practice of internationally recognized human rights was far from institutionalized. And where one finds civil war and/ or a situation close to genocide, there may be even more fundamental rights violations than under the later stages of communism.

Even for states like the former binational state of Czechoslovakia, as well as Hungary and Poland, all of which were trying to move rapidly toward democratic state-capitalism, the problems of transition from communism to a hoped-for rights-protective regime were considerable. Perhaps the chief problem is the sad state of their economies after years of command from the party-state apparatus. Even in the long-standing stable democracies of the West, many citizens seem more interested in the pursuit of prosperity than in civil and political rights witness low turnout for voting and a willingness to suppress the rights of those on the opposite side of an issue. Many are the democracies like Weimar Germany, not to mention those in Latin America, that have fallen in large part because of the perceived mismanagement of the economy by the government.

Mark Gibney recalls that even in the mild economic slump in the capitalist West during the late I980s and early I990s, there was an increased search for scapegoats and a tendency to take out frustrations on "foreigners." The right-wing fringe groups have been especially violent in the unified Germany, although public opinion polls showed that about

85 percent of all Germans opposed the violent attacks on asylum seekers. Especially in France there has been a right-wing backlash against immigrants from North Africa. More broadly speaking, we know that economic hard times lead to an increased willingness to tolerate radical authoritarian "solutions" to those problems; witness much middle-class support, at least initially, for the dictator Pinochet in Chile and the military junta in Argentina (and in Brazil previously).

Vaclav Trojan has wittily remarked that communism represents the longest way from crude capitalism back to crude capitalism, before one might arrive at progressive state capitalism with a moderating welfare system. If so, states like the Czech Republic, Hungary, and Poland may have to try to endure the problems produced by a quest for pure economic growth, in the hope that eventually one could moderate the rougher edges of capitalism such as job insecurity in the long run. We should recall that the International Bill of Rights entails the socio-economic rights to education, holidays with pay, social security, adequate nutrition, clothing, shelter, and health care. Even some champions of the Reagan administrations, known for their quasi-religious belief in the miracles of unregulated private markets, acknowledged that the dynamism of capitalism was accompanied by considerable harshness for those who did not benefit from laissez-faire capitalism.

Whether various peoples like the Poles would endure a relatively harsh transitional phase, during which the economy would hopefully become more globally competitive, without rejecting the democratic part of the equation, remains to be seen. One of the splits in federal Czechoslovakia was over whether one should move ahead with difficult economic privatization as quickly as possible, as favored in the Czech lands, or continue with relatively large governmental subsidies and other cushions, as favored in Slovakia. In other countries, such as Japan, many citizens had agreed to go without many consumer comforts for several decades for the sake of the national economy as a whole. Whether such sentiments would prevail in Eastern Europe could not be known for sure. After forty to seventy years of communism in the Soviet bloc, there was considerable reluctance to engage in entrepreneurship and competition. Indeed, some historians have reminded us that even before 1917, capitalism did not have the same favorable image in parts of the Russian empire that it did in most parts of the West. Gorbachev found out, as a Czech intellectual later remarked, that when the doors of the communist "zoo" were opened, many of the "animals" feared the freedom of the capitalist "jungle."

It is at least somewhat encouraging that Hungary, in particular, had considerable experience with private markets during its version of "goulash communism," and that other states, like Poland, were trying to make economic efficiency one of their primary goals.

It should also be recalled, however, that difficult economic times do not always undermine internationally recognized civil and political rights. Both Botswana and Zimbabwe managed to protect a broad range of rights despite considerable economic difficulties. Sri Lanka likewise did well for a decade or so after independence, until the conflict between the Sri Lankan Tamils and the Sinhalese Buddhists, crosscut by other conflicts, destabilized the country. Democratic Argentina has endured not just hyper-inflation but also a series of coups and even some resurgence of terrorism, without yet sliding back into military rule. Costa Rica and a number of states in the Caribbean have been able to implement many human rights despite lack of national affluence.

If the political attitudes of a people determine the status of human rights practice, we are still not sure what really produces the elite tolerance and other values that underline a stable rights-protective regime. We can venture explanations as to why the situation is different in Romania from that in the Czech lands, for example, but we must admit that we still cannot predict precisely the evolution of human rights considerations. We are not alone in this limitation.

International Factors

By and large the international factors at work on the situation in the former Soviet bloc have been secondary rather than primary for the fate of human rights. Nevertheless, in various situations some of the international efforts have generated a moderate degree of influence. In his introductory chapter, Donnelly suggested certain steps that the U. S. and others could take to advance the practice of rights in foreign states, without unduly raising expectations about what can be achieved. Donnelly, comparing the optimism immediately after the collapse of Stalinism with the slow building of a rights-protective regime, stressed the benchmarks of severity of rights violations, trends over time in rights protection, the responsibility of outside states for the situation, and concentrating on what can be achieved.

Congressman Doug Bereuter showed that the United States had indeed done something about human rights in the new Europe, although he acknowledged that budgetary concerns made, and will continue to make, the U. S. commitment modest as it concentrates on the practical modalities of implementing civil and political rights. Moreover, consistent with developments in Eastern Europe already noted in the previous section, Congressman Bereuter does not expect a simple export of the U. S. model of democracy, but rather believes the U. S. should defer to whatever democratic structures and leaders emerge from local politics. Bereuter's views fit well with a body of academic thought suggesting that particular models of democracy are not exportable, even though democracy in general might be promoted by foreign actors.

Raphael Zariski showed quite clearly that some of the West European states, such as Britain, have not had an activist policy toward the East, whether concerning human rights or other subject matter. Some others, such as Germany or Italy, which is concerned with states close to it, are playing a much greater role. Zariski's theme is well taken: all outside states are pursuing a variety of interests and concerns in the East, and human rights considerations make up only part of each state's foreign policy agenda. Donnelly agrees on this point. And the editor notes that some West European states have tended to either shift or dump human rights issues into multilateral institutions.

Nevertheless, both Zariski and Gibney emphasize that the fate of human rights in the East has a direct bearing on West European states. Both make clear that economic failure, repression, and political instability will generate large migratory flows with concomitant pressures on, and problems for, the West. This situation is most clear concerning Germany, which has had a relatively generous asylum policy toward foreigners fleeing not just individual persecution but also instability and war. We have already noted a violent backlash by 1992 against this generous German asylum policy.

Gibney is quite correct in arguing that if Western states took a greater interest in correcting the human rights abuses giving rise to various types of refugees, they would not be faced with so many asylum seekers. Yet, like the United States in its relations with Haiti, many western states, in dealing with the East, pursued reactive policies regarding immigration rather than anticipatory problems dealing with human rights, which were frequently at the heart of migration flows.

While no individual Western state was eager to tackle Eastern problems on its own (although Germany made the clearest attempt), no multilateral institution was able to make a major impact on the Eastern situation either at least not by early 1993.

The United Nations Security Council, as propelled by its major Western member states, was certainly deeply involved in both attempted peacemaking and traditional peacekeeping activities. As the editor showed in his chapter, UN peacekeeping in the former greater Yugoslavia had helped fighting parties disengage along the Serbian Croation borders and around the airport in Sarajevo. Yet the council had not manifested the political will to decisively deal with the underlying causes of violence in the Balkans, much less in several parts of the former Soviet Union that manifested armed conflict of various sorts. Peacemaking had been attempted especially through using former U. S. Secretary of State Cyrus Vance as a special envoy, but without decisive results in the short run. The UN Human Rights Commission had appointed a special envoy to address human rights issues in the Balkans, but again without decisive results.

Even more so had other multilateral institutions failed to ameliorate to any great extent the social, economic, and political problems plaguing the East. It was somewhat ironic that the CSCE process had found a greater niche for itself in dealing with human rights during the cold war than in helping protect rights thereafter. But the CSCE lacked both the military and economic muscle that was apparently needed to reign in, particularly, the ethnic passions of the Balkans and southern sections of the former Soviet Union. There were a variety of CSCE demarches concerning human rights during 1989-92, but without decisive results.

Likewise, the presumed magnet and moderating influence of the EC seemed irrelevant to those who elevated the settling of old passionate grievances over rational calculation of future economic benefits. Extremists in Serbia, Azerbaijan, Armenia, Georgia, and elsewhere seemed not to care about the possibility of economic support from the West in the future. Unlike in other polities, the pursuit of economic prosperity took second place or even lower to emotional and symbolic politics.

Given the demise of the Soviet Union, if NATO and/or the West European Union (WEU) could not devise a role for themselves in counteracting violence in the Balkans in particular, one had to wonder what was their role after the cold war. Since they were no longer needed for either deterrence or fighting vis-à-vis the Soviet bloc, what was their raison d'être if not for peacekeeping, enforcement, or humanitarian police action? Yet neither organization had been brought into decisive action by early 1993.

Underlying the weakness of multilateral institutions was the apathy by, and disagreement among, their member states. As Zariski noted, multilateral arrangements mostly reflect the policies of member states. Even at the United Nations, with a secretary general in the person of Boutros Boutros Ghali of Egypt, who was prone to activism, even of an abrasive kind, his would-be leadership was constrained by member states' policies particularly those of the permanent members of the Security Council.

There was a certain West European traditional pessimism and cynicism at work, a belief that the situation in the East would only improve when the various major players had exhausted themselves or come to dominate their neighbors. In the meantime, in this view, there was no major interest on the part of the West Europeans propelling decisive intervention, particularly of the forcible kind. For Germany in particular, this was a highly debatable notion. Had Germany been able to provide greater leadership on eastern questions (although its involvement was greater than that of its neighbors), Germany would not have been racked by such violence against foreigners. It is a fair question whether the internal peace of Germany was an "interest" sufficient to justify more pressure for an end to human rights violations in much of the East.

The U. S. commitment to correcting major human rights abuses in the new Europe was slight, despite the more mundane programs mentioned by Doug Bereuter. The United States made periodic public relations gestures, such as having the UN Security Council adopt a resolution (S/Res/770) authorizing all necessary means to ensure humanitarian assistance in Bosnia. But when it came to Serbian policies like ethnic cleansing and military attacks on civilian targets, the United States by early 1993 had done little more than endorse diplomacy backed by economic sanctions. Donnelly was all too correct when he noted that moral interdependence was still weak, and that even when it was present, most states were unwilling to pay high material and other costs to correct even gross violations of rights in other states.

If we broaden the picture, we can note that the United States did not gear up to do anything about massive starvation in Somalia, a former cold-war ally, until late August 1992. The International Committee of the Red Cross, with extensive operations in that country, had been warning of the human disaster, in reality a gross violation of both civil and socio-economic rights, from February 1992. The United Nations had endorsed that warning.

Even in the spring of 1991, when the United States undertook military action presumably on behalf of the rights of Iraqi citizens, especially the Kurds, it was not until media coverage in Western Europe, and resulting action by the British and French governments, that the U. S. government moved on that issue. And when the United States reversed policy and projected its military into the south of Iraq in August I992, many observers speculated that the reasons seemed to have more to do with putting pressure on Sadam Hussein (if not with the U. S. presidential election that fall) than with any genuine concern for the rights of the Shi'ites in the south of Iraq especially since their rights had been ignored by the United States previously.

Against this broadened backdrop, U. S. policy on rights questions in the new Europe was part of a broader orientation. That U. S. orientation was a denigration of the semantics of a new world order. U. S. policies only showed that there was no substance to the rhetoric. If anything, they showed that the old world disorder prevailed. Washington, like its counterparts in Western Europe, in reality deferred to "facts on the ground." The fate of human rights was being left to internal or local or regional forces, many of them negative for the practice of rights, while the United States and other outsiders engaged in cynical diplomatic pretense. Aside from a fixation with Iraq, the United States only acted for rights, as in Somalia, when the public pressure became intolerable. Otherwise, U. S. officials spoke of the need to avoid another Vietnam-like quagmire, while being ready, of course, to take partial military measures in Iraq.

It may turn out to be the case that international economic sanctions on Serbia, made mandatory by the UN Security Council, will either be moderately influential or even decisive in curtailing Serbian policies violative of rights in the Balkans. It is at least possible that Western foreign assistance, either bilaterally or through the World Bank, not to mention the European Bank for Reconstruction and Development, will turn out to be moderately influential on the practice of rights in Russia. Thus we should not say that foreign or international factors are irrelevant for the practice of rights. In the broader perspective, we should note that international humanitarian assistance has made a difference in several situations in which social and economic rights were being grossly violated situations like Ethiopia in the mid-I980s and Somalia, finally, in the fall of 1992.

Nevertheless, we still must conclude that the practice of rights in the new Europe will usually be only moderately affected by international factors. It is paradoxical that while there has been a great increase in diplomatic attention to human rights in international relations particularly over the past quarter of a century, the actual practice of rights is still largely determined by factors within the territorial state. Spasmodic international action to guarantee the protection of human rights, as for the Iraqi Kurds or starving Somali, will be institutionalized only with difficulty and over time.

Turbulent Tensions

James N. Rosenau has argued that we live in a turbulent world characterized by a large number of interdependent actors, a great deal of political volatility, and competing norms and values. If that is true, and certainly Rosenau's version is close to the truth, it is no wonder that explanation and prediction is so difficult in international relations whether pertaining to human rights or to any other issue area.

In addition to the great variety and mix of factors involved in the successful practice of human rights in the 1990s, there are two additional methodological problems worthy of note. First, as often remarked, we should recall that few, if any, scholars or public officials predicted with any precision the remarkable transformations in European communism during the period 1985-91. In part this is because of the unpredictable role of individuals in world affairs. Mikhail Gorbachev had risen through the communist ranks in his native Soviet Union as a loyal devote of the party-state system. So had Boris Yeltsin. So had Eduard Schevemadze. From the point of view of 1984, there was little if any evidence that any of these three, or many others, were in favor of radical change within the Union of Soviet Socialist Republics or would be in favor of new states to replace the Union of Soviet Socialist Republics. The pattern of behavior constituting the basis for prediction did not allow a projection of what was to transpire.

The same was true for Anwar Sadat in Egypt. He had acted as a loyal and unthreatening second in command to Gamal Nasser for years. He had not sought, nor had he exercised, independence and creativity. Yet upon replacing Nasser, Sadat became one of the more creative leaders of his time, taking risks for peace with Israel that in no way could have been projected from his public life before the events unfolded.

The same could be said of John Kennedy in the Cuban missile crisis of 1962. Given his past indecisive and lacklustre decisions pertaining to the Bay of Pigs invasion, the building of the Berlin wall, and the debate with Khruschev, there was simply no basis for prediction that he would be firm, daring, and creative in his determination to see the Soviet attack missiles removed from Castro's Cuba.

And so it is with the future of human rights in the new Europe. In I989 it was impossible to predict that Meciar in Slovakia would emerge as a political leader, using the issue of Slovak independence to propel himself to high office. In 1989 it was impossible to predict that Gamsakhurdia in Georgia would show such traits of inflexibility and lack of tolerance that Georgia was plunged into civil war. Would former communist leaders in Bulgaria or the Ukraine turn out to be committed to rights principles? Would a Boris Yeltsin emerge in Moldavia or Romania?To be sure, as we have tried to suggest in this concluding chapter, there are certain historical trends and global patterns that give us some basis for *general* prediction about internationally recognized human rights. For example, as we said, where there is economic growth with equitable distribution of benefits, a growing middle class, widespread education, experience with democracy in local politics, and stable leadership transfers, there is a reasonable basis to predict greater success in the practice of many universal human rights. But beneath that general level of predicting probabilities, the variability of human perspectives and decision making makes precise prediction a very risky business. But, and this brings us to our second methodological problem in prediction beyond turbulence and human variability, a number of situations are characterized by conflicting factors rather than one clear trend. The result is a tension between factors, or perhaps an overall paradoxical situation. Where such tensions obtain, evolution of the situation can develop in one of several directions, again defying prediction. Consider the following tensions or paradoxes in the new Europe:

- As Donnelly noted, we have optimism over the collapse of Leninist systems of rule, but pessimism over the dictatorial and chauvinistic systems that sometimes replaced them.
- As the editor observed, we have confusion in the number of actors, including multilateral institutions, trying to influence the practice of rights in the new Europe, but this confusion allows for many possible diplomatic demarches, some of which may turn out to be at least moderately successful.
- As Hollander pointed out, quoting Dostoyevsky, "People long to be free but at the same time are afraid of what that freedom might bring."
- As Donnelly and Trojan noted, in several states there was a consensus in favor of rejecting communism, but there was disagreement over exactly how to treat past communist officials and party members and those who had cooperated with, and been secret informers for, the ancien régime.
- As Zariski and Donnelly emphasized, there may be more talk about human rights across borders, but states still tend to elevate economic and security interests to positions of priority on foreign policy agendas.
- As Hibbing explained, polities may make impressive starts in implementing the right of political participation, but then economic difficulties may cause citizens to bypass legislatures and other established policy-making organs in quest of extra-constitutional solutions to their problems.

Such tensions, conflicts, and paradoxes bedevil the social sciences and their attempts to precisely chart the future. What we can say for sure, and what this volume has clearly shown is the following: Most of the new states in the new Europe accept the principles of democratic state capitalism in a form consistent with internationally recognized human rights, yet only some of them, particularly in East Central

Europe, are making rapid progress in institutionalizing the stable practice of those rights;

1. Historical, cultural, social, and economic factors particular to the new states of the new Europe will primarily determine the future of the practice of human rights; only a few states, again those in East Central Europe and perhaps a few other selected areas, show the combination of factors that has increased serious attention to human rights in polities like Taiwan and South Korea;
2. While most states are increasingly under some international pressure to comply with internationally recognized human rights, this pressure varies from state to state, situation to situation, and era to era; a growth in international diplomacy for human rights is not always backed by a determined and sometimes costly international effort to go beyond lip service to human rights norms;
3. Finally, while there has been considerable progress in advancing the practice of human rights in many parts of the new Europe, the problems impeding that practice are sufficient to cause us to be extremely cautious about the future of rights in this part of the world; to close our circle, we repeat Donnelly's early point that the collapse of one form of repression and exploitation is not the same as the construction of a rights-protective governing system in its place.

8

"Velvet Revolutions" in East Central Europe for Human Rights

Introduction

The pervasiveness of such demands can be traced in part to the fact that, unlike violent and protracted conflicts, the "velvet revolutions" left the "vanquished" Communists alive and well, with their privileges virtually intact. A thorough settling of accounts with the old regime, however, has proved not only complex but potentially dangerous. For example, calls for prosecution of the old guard have jeopardized coalition rule in Poland and Hungary. Meanwhile, velvet revolutionaries in Germany and Czechoslovakia have grappled with contradictions between rule of law and purge. Vaclav Havel, the first post Communist President of Czechoslovakia, described his nation's law on screening state institutions for former secret police collaborators as "a somewhat revolutionary law, a law that is attempting to do something from above that our society failed to do and did not have the strength to do from below."

I am investigating how new Central European democracies are coping with the legacies of Communist rule. I argue that the nature of the antecedent regime and the kind of transition to democracy exert considerable influence on the options and pressures facing new regimes. Thus, I begin by outlining the extent and forms of repression employed under Communist rule. Second, I address the types of transitions from communism and their consequences for new regimes in terms of breaking with the past. After examining the concrete issues and practical obstacles that have arisen in terms of "settling accounts" in post-Communist states, I assess the efficacy of government policies in accomplishing professed aims. To illustrate the process of de-communization, I analyze the most advanced case thus far, that of pre-1993Czechoslovakia. After comparing Czechoslovakia's wide-ranging efforts to the strategies employed in Poland, Hungary, and the former German Democratic Republic, or GDR, I speculate on the lessons of East Central Europe for other nations that are struggling with the legacies of repressive rule.

From Repression to Revolt

In Eastern Europe the excesses and injustices under Communist rule began with the postwar takeovers themselves. The revolution mandated expropriation and *etatization* of private property. Moreover, in accordance with Soviet directives, "building communism" included liquidation of class enemies and constant vigilance against counterrevolutionaries, especially within the Communist parties themselves. The Soviet-style "replica regimes" not only reproduced the command economic system but also adopted the brutal methods employed by Stalin and his secret police to suppress real and potential opposition. In East Germany former Nazi concentration camps soon housed new political prisoners, and across the Soviet bloc show trials resulted in death or imprisonment for hundreds of thousands of people.

Stalin's death in 1953 opened a new era in East European politics. A waning of brutality and repression, as well as a rise in public expression of discontent and unrest, characterized this phase of "destalinization." Khrushchev's 1956 denunciation of Stalin's crimes and miscalculations sent shock waves through Eastern Europe. It raised the issue of reforming the political and economic system and revealed the fallibility of Moscow. While each Eastern bloc nation followed a distinct course of experimentation with liberalization, all were characterized by what J. F. Brown calls a tension between "viability" and "cohesion" that is, pressure for national domestic efficacy versus the demand for conformity with central Soviet domestic and foreign policy. The two most striking manifestations of this unresolvable tension were the 1956 Hungarian revolution and the 1968 Prague Spring reforms, both of which made sharp rejections of Stalinist brutalities and purges part of their campaigns for legitimacy before being crushed by Soviet military intervention. Indeed, during its brief "thaw," Czechoslovakia adopted the "only law on rehabilitations in postwar Eastern Europe." Restoration of conservative Communist rule cut short efforts to restore justice to the victims of Stalinist purges. Nevertheless, although the failed revolutions generated a second series of purges to punish the rebels and discourage potential radicals, the arbitrariness and mass executions associated with Stalinism had ended.

In the wake of failed radical reform, the East European Communist regimes engaged in a particular form of counterreformation that is, they offered their citizens an improved standard of living and some economic freedom in exchange for an end to political pluralism and meaningful political participation. Repression did not end, but it took on less visible and more predictable forms. As one Czechoslovak dissident described the effects of the new system:

> *At some point in their life everyone had to make an agonizing choice: to prove their loyalty to the regime by humiliating themselves*

or to lose everything. Everybody knew what "everything" meant. It meant to lose not only your own career, but to blight the future of your children, because they would not be allowed to attend university.

Despite the milder nature of their sanctions against dissidents, the East European Communist regimes continued to strive for total control and therefore blocked the functioning of any civil society. Not only intellectuals but vast numbers of citizens from all walks of life were recruited often through blackmail to become informers for the secret police. Sophisticated police networks kept tabs on all strata of society but persecuted only those individuals who overtly expressed their dissatisfaction or disagreement with the regime. Yet at the same time the regime made real neutrality impossible. In his sophisticated analysis of the dynamics of totalitarianism, Havel has explained how, by extracting constant professions of loyalty, the Communist regime created the image of unanimity and simultaneously made its citizens complicit in the propping up of the Communist system. The majority of the population of the Eastern bloc surrendered to the demands of the regime and channeled their energy into their private, material lives. The few open dissenters responded to the counterreformation by abandoning the tactic of trying to reform the regime and instead advocating construction of a "second society" or "parallel polis" that is, reform of one's own life space regardless of one's inability to affect high politics directly. The success of dissidents in creating an independent civil society varied widely from the mass Solidarity movement that united workers and intellectuals in Poland to tiny networks of intellectual and religious dissidents in Hungary and East Germany.

The Path of Velvet Revolution

Economic crisis, which had been building in East Central Europe throughout the 1970s, blossomed into breakdown in the late 1980s under the stimulus of Soviet leader Mikhail Gorbachev's dual domestic and foreign reform programs.

Gorbachev's domestic economic and political liberalization proposals fueled the efforts of liberal Communists in Eastern Europe to reform their own systems; thus the split in the Soviet Communist Party reproduced itself elsewhere. Moreover, Gorbachev's "new thinking" about global cooperation produced the "Sinatra doctrine," which in contrast to the "Brezhnev doctrine" coined during the Prague Spring to formalize the Soviet prerogative to intervene in the case of breakdowns of Communist orthodoxy in Eastern Europe allowed the Warsaw Pact countries to "do it their way."

Not surprisingly, Poland with its highly developed opposition Solidarity movement first exploited the breakdown of authority to displace its Communist leaders. After the Polish regime failed to win even a minimal level of popular support, in 1989 it entered into round-table talks with the opposition. The resulting compromise set free elections for a newly created upper house of the parliament the senate and for 35 percent of seats in the lower house the Sjem. It also stipulated parliamentary election of a president, who would be granted broad powers. The June 1989 parliamentary elections left the Communist Party and its puppet coalition partners with their guaranteed 65 percent of the seats in the Sjem and a single seat out of the 100 places in the upper house. As had been agreed, the new cabinet allowed the Communists to fill the posts of minister of defense and minister of interior. On the whole, however, its devastating defeat cast the Communist Party into such a decline that even its hold on the Sjem disintegrated, allowing Solidarity an almost free hand in economic reform.

The Hungarian Communist Party similarly moved from confrontation to compromise to collapse. In this instance, the post-1956 conservative leadership had managed to coexist peacefully with Moscow and with its own cowed citizenry. Encouraged by Gorbachev's perestroika and frightened by signs of Hungary's own economic decline, however, beginning in 1988 frustrated reformers within the

Communist Party began to shake up the hierarchy. The reformers then moved to shore up popular support by formulating plans to reform the economy and to "'constitutionalize' public life." The regime, in effect, legitimized the opposition which unlike Solidarity consisted of several relatively small organizations by inviting them to participate in a series of talks about radical economic change. The Hungarian round-table talks ran from mid-June to mid-September 1989, and the opposition, though fragmented, refused to be limited to discussing economic measures alone. It too won considerable concessions, including free presidential and parliamentary elections. In the March 1990 elections various opposition parties won nearly 85 percent of the seats.

In mid- 1989, as their neighbors tested the limits of political reform, Czechoslovakia and East Germany still appeared to be solidly under the sway of unwavering Communist regimes. Czechoslovak and GDR hard-liners dominated their organizations and had neither compromised with dissidents nor flirted with glasnost and democratization. East German identity as a separate state has been grounded in its promise of *socialist* economic success and its practice of gradual political liberalization; in the 1980s it became clear to many citizens that neither of these trends was progressing as expected. As one analyst observed: "Honecker raised expectations, Gorbachev hijacked them." East German leaders could not sacrifice their socialist orientation easily, but many GDR citizens showed less restraint. In the summer of 1989 many GDR residents took advantage of unrestricted travel to their more liberalized bloc allies to flee to West Germany. While shaken by this hemorrhage of refugees, the East German regime was ultimately toppled by massive street protests by those who stayed behind. The Communist Party, unable to produce a viable reformist leader to negotiate with the opposition, finally gave way to a weak coalition regime that would orchestrate the end of East Germany as a nation.

Czechoslovak leaders had their own specific reasons to fear Gorbachev's push for liberalization. Glasnost would undoubtedly raise the issue of the 1968 invasion and produce a postmortem that was bound to reflect badly on the conservative leadership, which still held the posts it had gained through the crushing of the reform movement. As in East Germany, the rising tide of change in the Socialist bloc raised the expectations of the populace. Here too, massive, unprecedented popular protests catalyzed the collapse of the Communist regime. In Czechoslovakia a strong dissident movement, relatively untouched by emigration, provided leadership for popular protest through Civic Forum in the Czech lands and Public against Violence in Slovakia. Use of violence against student demonstrators on November 17, 1989 further discredited the regime and inspired public reaction. For the first time workers joined dissidents in a two-hour general strike. Deprived of this base of passive acquiescence, if not support, the government scrambled to devolve political control peacefully. On December 29, the Federal Assembly unanimously chose Havel as the nation's new president, with free parliamentary elections to follow.

Dimensions of "Settling Accounts" with Communism

In the rapid, nonviolent demise of communism one can find both a source of popular elation and optimism as well as seeds of coming frustration. The two major forms of regime change, pact and protest, *nowhere overturned the majority of power structures of the old regime.* Although the democratic oppositions obviously took over parliamentary and high executive posts, this altered only the tip of the iceberg of Communist domination. Top Communist officials had resigned their political posts, but what of the Communist Party's immense financial assets and properties? What of all the managers, administrators, and civil servants that had executed the old regime's commands? The secret police obviously needed to be purged and restructured, but what about other institutions and their staffs? Moreover, no "revolutionary justice" had been meted out against the old regimes. New governments had to sort out and decide the fate of all levels of participants in the old regime. Essentially, three major questions regarding settling accounts with the old Communist regimes erupted during and after the democratic transitions: institutional reform, reparations to victims, and screening and/or prosecution of collaborators and criminals. Whereas these issues are common to transitions from repressive rule, the extent, duration, and intensity of Communist penetration of politics, society, and the economy as well as the "soft" nature of the transitions make settling accounts particularly complex.

First, as regards "institutional reform," a thorough overhaul could conceivably encompass a huge variety of organizations, from universities to the military to the completely state-run media. Beginning with political structures, democratization required stripping the Communist Party of its position as final arbiter over all policy making and making it subject to rule of law. Departyization entailed not just personnel changes but creation of new structures of accountability within the army, police, and judiciary to make them subordinate to elected officials rather than to the party hierarchy. Under communism the term *nomenklatura* was invented to refer to the enormous list of local and central cultural, political, and economic posts where hiring was subject to Communist Party confirmation. All of these jobs now had to be filled by other means, but changing selection procedures could have little effect unless these posts were first vacated.

Prosecution of those guilty of committing clear criminal offenses under the law is contentious, but legally purging bureaucrats requires great ingenuity and daring. "Fair" screening of personnel entails resolution of numerous complex problems. Agreement must be reached on standards for evaluation of culpability; procedures for this evaluation, including a decision on who is to be evaluated and by whom;

and a set of graduated sanctions. The extent of Communist Party control exposed a huge number of people to accusations of responsibility for crimes ranging from economic mismanagement and environmental destruction to mistreatment of political prisoners and embezzlement of state funds. In this respect, the situation in Eastern Europe is more like that of postwar France than of former authoritarian regimes in Latin America. This is so because the most frequent charge is not violation of human rights but "collaboration" which is not only hard to define but problematic because prosecution of such an offense frequently relies on assumptions of "collective guilt" and employs ex post facto laws.

Finally, just as it is problematic to identify who is responsible for the many "evils of communism," it is equally difficult to decide who should be considered a victim and subsequently what should be done about compensation. Again, some cases seem fairly clear-cut that is, those imprisoned without trial or fired for political reasons merit legal rehabilitation if not reinstatement. But what about those who were barred from higher education, denied work in their field of specialization, or blackmailed by the secret police? And given the general economic devastation left by Communist rule, how can the state now expect to take money from the general public to make amends for injustices that cannot be corrected by any sum of money?

Rather than speculate on possible resolutions to these questions in the abstract, I will use the case of Czechoslovakia to show how one post-Communist regime has struggled to address these issues simultaneously. I focus on Czechoslovakia because it has produced a wide range of debates and compromises on institutional reform, screening, and reparations. I will then briefly contrast Czech approaches to official attempts to come terms with the past in other East Central European nations. While events have continued unfolding, this account focuses on the period before the January 1993 division of Czechoslovakia into two separate states.

Czechoslovak Approach to Settling Accounts with Communists

Czechoslovakia did not quickly succumb to democratization or perestroika. Indeed, the regime continued to persecute dissidents up until the November revolution. Despite decades of pressure, Czechoslovak dissidents, primarily through the Charter 77 organization, had built a strong reputation for integrity and anticommunism. In the days of the revolution dissidents led the broad popular opposition movements, thus cementing their status as democrats and leaders. Playwright Vaclav Havel, the nation's most famous dissident, was overwhelmingly chosen to head the new government. Havel brought with him tremendous moral authority and a particular ethical view of culpability for totalitarian rule. His initial stance might be labeled forgiveness without forgetting. In an early address to the nation, Havel argued that whereas one should not forget either the martyrs or the murderers, accounts should be settled on the pages of history books; in practice, forgiveness was the best policy. Resorting to witch hunts meant accepting the mistaken principle employed by the Communists that the ends justify the means. In this same speech, Havel admitted that the federal government nevertheless faced difficulties in regard to the transition:

> *We live in a peculiar and paradoxical time. We are building a legal state, so to speak, in a revolutionary way. Due to this an emphasis on the law is impeding and frustrating the revolution from time to time, while contrarily the revolutionary nature of things flouts the law from time to time.*

Havel proposed to remedy this dilemma with quick and energetic work by the parliament to set up a "normally functioning democracy." Such optimism about a rapid, relatively painless break with the past was justified in Havel's opinion because "the totalitarian system has fallen and its structures if they still exist at all are in the service of new times, or are paralyzed to such an extent that they cannot achieve anything more than mud stirring." Havel's approach, while fitting his own moral philosophy, proved somewhat naive and did not satisfy many citizens.

Examples of Institutional Reform: Police, Judiciary, Industry, and Party

Democratic reformers made the dismantling of the secret police one of their first objectives. While admitting that every state needs a counterintelligence agency, the democrats sought to disarm the mechanisms of internal repression, embodied primarily in the State Security apparat (StB). The first new minister of internal affairs was Richard Sacher, a compromise candidate from the Catholic People's Party. (This party was one of several puppet organizations allowed to exist after the Communist takeover as part of a façade of pluralism.) Under the old regime the ministry of internal affairs had 18,000 employees and relied on a network of over 140,000 informers to spy on a population of 15 million. Sacher promised to cut the overall number of staff to 6,000 and to carefully screen all employees. Many democrats, however, perceived Sacher as moving slowly and hesitantly. They criticized him for abolishing the StB altogether only after pressure from Civic Forum. Further, the public expressed dissatisfaction about the six months of compensation pay received by fired StB employees. More damaging to Sacher, however, were revelations that he had gone to great trouble to find a new post for former deputy minister of internal affairs Alojz Lorenc who was later indicted on three criminal charges, including destruction of StB archive materials and that he had loosed a smear campaign against a Civic Forum member who had strongly criticized him. Finally, Sacher's own deputies accused him of ordering investigations into the activities of current government and parliamentary leaders. The furor over the choice of a reluctant reformer to hold this sensitive position led Havel to replace Sacher with former Charter 77 spokesman Jiri Ruml in the summer of 1990. Even Ruml, however, became entangled in controversy over his position when he released information gained from secret police files that a leader of the People's Party, and candidate for parliament, had been a long-time secret police informer.

Most institutional reform, however, could not be achieved by razing old organizations and starting from scratch. In the restructuring of the judiciary one finds a more typical situation: Some parts of the institution were compromised by their service under the old regime, but the majority of departments contained professional, hard-to-replace specialists. Thus, overhauling the judiciary required positive restructuring as well as some housecleaning. Parliament intervened slowly and incrementally to increase judges' independence and to expand judicial purview. In July 1991, for instance, it created commercial and administrative courts to supplement civil and criminal courts and to handle a whole range of legal activity that had not existed under communism.

Reorganization alone, however, could not address the main obstacle to restoring trust in the legal system the judges themselves. Those judges who had presided over political trials inspired disdain, whereas those who had granted special treatment to the Communist elite were open to blackmail. Beyond providing incentives to recruit new judges, the government began a case-by-case screening of judges already on the bench. This individualized and time-consuming process was stipulated by law judges were elected for ten-year terms subject to recall only on "serious grounds." A July 1991 law, in an effort to retain and attract capable judges, finally mandated that henceforth all judges except those on the constitutional court would be appointed for life, but that all those appointed before January 1, 1990 had to be reappointed within the next twelve months if they were to continue in the judiciary. This vetting, however, targeted only those guilty of blatant collaboration, not those who had been informers or secret police agents (the comprehensive screening law that further affects the judiciary is discussed below). With regard to criminal prosecution of judges and prosecutors involved in trying and sentencing dissidents, including Havel, the prosecutor general rejected this as incompatible with the "ethical revolution which proclaims love and forgiveness." The most visible result of all these reform efforts thus far has been a shortage of judges because of voluntary resignations and purges, accompanied by a surge of claims resulting from new rehabilitation and property-restitution laws.

The problem of whether and how to replace experienced personnel also arises in regard to reforming the economy. Popular expectations that Communist dominance in the management of state enterprises would decline dramatically after the first free elections in June 1990 were sorely disappointed. Conflict over the necessity and means for turnover in management rapidly peaked when in July 1990 a local branch of Civic Forum produced a list of 250 top managers in its district and identified over half as Communists. The government protested that the only conceivable use for such a list was a purge based on political beliefs, whereas the criterion for judging managers should be how well they performed their jobs. Civic Forum responded that the predominance of Communist appointees made for a "Communist mafia" that used its position not only to discriminate against non-Communists but to block economic reform and subvert privatization in order to enrich themselves. In an August speech, Havel recognized these concerns about replacing managers and spoke of the need for a "second revolution"; however, he argued that rapid market reform and privatization, not an administrative purge, would best replace bad managers. Thus, Havel reflected the government's twofold concerns: that the already troubled economy not fall into the hands of incompetent amateurs and that democratic principles and individual rights be respected.

Popular resentment over decades of state surveillance and political misrule extended beyond the specific institutions that executed policy to the single institution responsible for policy making the Communist Party. In many minds, the party bore the blame for past and present problems, from violating individual human rights to pollution and economic crisis. In the debates over the party's fate, propositions ranged from banning the party outright as many West European nations banned fascist parties after World War II to confiscating its assets and/or putting its leaders on trial. Havel held firm that the principle of political pluralism should not be sacrificed unless the reconstituted Communist Party violated the constitution. Others argued that the Communist Party had never been a political party in the normal sense of the word and hence should not be treated as such. As one former dissident put it:

> There's been a fatal confusion of two things: the right of demagogic parties to exist, and the right to proceed with the transmogrification of a particular mafia organization called the Communist Party. The Communist Party should be abolished, and its assets should be confiscated as symbolic recompense for wrongs committed. Its elected members of parliament could then form some sort of new party to represent the preposterous left.

In the spring of 1990, the Confederation of Political Prisoners mobilized some twenty thousand demonstrators to support a local prosecutor who had been reprimanded for initiating an investigation of the Communist Party for violating laws against spreading fascism, and seventy thousand people signed a petition of hunger strikers calling for banning the party. Finally, in October 1990, the Federal Assembly passed a law nationalizing party property, though by this time the party's assets had shrunk by over half since the revolution as party functionaries siphoned off what they could. (Prose cutions for bribery, embezzlement, and misuse of state funds are proceeding on an individual basis.) Despite the precipitous decline in the size and strength of the

Communist Party, the government continued to chip away at the party, outlawing the propagation of fascism and communism in cases where they violate human rights.

Compensation and Reparations

The new democratic government moved quickly to rehabilitate and compensate former political prisoners. In April 1990, the Federal Assembly passed a law on judicial rehabilitation that provided for the outright annulment of verdicts in convictions for political crimes. Beginning in July 1990, former prisoners or their heirs could turn to the courts for rehabilitation. Upon receipt of a certificate of rehabilitation they could apply, again through the courts, for compensation for lost wages, costs of legal defense, and of any fines paid. The state agreed to pay limited compensation in cash over the next ten years. By the end of 1991, 202,295 citizens had been rehabilitated, but of 37,805 claims for compensation only 7,374 had been settled because of the overburdening of the new commercial courts. Moreover, individual institutions ranging from the military to the patent office made provisions for those expelled for their political stances in 1968 to resume their old careers. The provisions of the law on judicial rehabilitation, however, have only partially satisfied the demands of the Confederation of Political Prisoners, which requests "decent pensions" and additional medical care, especially for persons who were exposed to uranium during forced hard labor. Moreover, no compensation existed for opportunities lost because of blacklists that barred people from studying or working in their professions.

Although compensation to former prisoners aroused little controversy, a tremendous dispute broke out in parliament over restitution to former property owners. An early bill restoring property nationalized between 1955 and 1961 passed fairly easily because its time limit meant it affected mainly small business and apartment house owners. When the Federal Assembly had to consider restitution for large businesses, however, fierce debate erupted over the form, extent, and subjects of restitution. Added pressure arose from the need to resolve the restitution question before privatization of large enterprises could be undertaken. The government was concerned that the costs of restitution would fall on taxpayers. A Slovak leader expressed his objections bluntly: "The past was cruel, but it was what it was. We cannot reconstruct the relations that existed in the past, and atonement understood this way is not possible." Yet most Czechs felt a moral obligation to make some compensation for lost property, and thus a compromise was reached that granted limited restitution. Although the Czechoslovaks are fortunate in having well-preserved records on property ownership, the danger of overwhelming litigation still looms, especially in cases involving property that has been improved over time. Moreover, more legislation is needed to address restoration of political parties' and Church property as well as restitution of land.

Screenings and Prosecutions

Along with calling for disbandment of the secret police, democratic revolutionaries early on demanded screening of top officials to detect secret police agents and collaborators. Actual vetting, however, has been not only prolonged but partial and painful. Some political parties and candidates in the parliamentary elections asked to be screened, but this ad hoc lustration relied on incomplete records and did not mandate disclosure of results. Thus, although deputies to the new parliament were democratically elected, doubts remained about their pasts. Widespread fear of hidden agents and blackmail, punctuated by sporadic scandals, led to a second stage of screening. Parliament had begun its term by setting up a commission to investigate the violence against demonstrators during the November revolution; it charged this commission with the delicate job of screening Federal Assembly deputies, the ministers and their deputies, as well as the employees of the presidential and Assembly offices. (Ironically, two members of an earlier task force to address the November events turned out to be secret police agents.) Collaborators in the ministries and offices could be fired, but deputies had parliamentary immunity and could not be forced to resign. Of the seventeen deputies found to have collaborated with the secret police, five resigned immediately; the others were publicly exposed, and several are now suing for defamation.

The second round of vetting satisfied neither those who wanted full disclosure nor those who believed the whole process was fatally flawed. Ultimately, however, public pressure pushed deputies toward more comprehensive legislation, and a federal screening law followed up efforts by Slovak and Czech National Councils. The national law applied to people who, between February 1948 and November 1989, were: members of the State Security Corps [StB]; are registered as StB resident agents, agents, holders of a rented conspiratorial apartment, informers, ideological collaborators, or conscious StB collaborators; secretaries of the Communist Party of Czechoslovakia [CPCZ] and the Communist Party of Slovakia [CPSL] bodies from district committees upward; members of the CPCZ and CPSL presidia from district committees upward; members of the CPCZ Central Committee, and the Central Committees of other republic-wide party bodies; those in the bodies who were involved in the political guidance of the National Security Corps; People's Militia members; members of Action Committees and screening commissions; and students of some military colleges in the USSR.

It bars these individuals, with the exception of those who held positions only during the Prague Spring period of 1968-69, from holding elected or appointed positions until 1996 in the following organizations:

> *state administration bodies, the Czechoslovak Army, the Federal Police Corps, the presidential office, the offices of the Federal Assembly, the Czech National Council and the Slovak National*

> *Council, the offices of all three governments, [state] radio and television, CSTK, state-owned enterprises, shareholding companies in which the state is the sole shareholder, foreign trade enterprises, budget funded and subsidized organizations, state funds, state-owned banks, the Czechoslovak State Bank, supreme judicial bodies, and the Czechoslovak Academy of Sciences and Slovak Academy of Sciences Presidiums.*

Anyone over the age of eighteen may apply under the law to receive a certificate verifying that he or she is not registered as an informant in the secret police files; and only with the consent of the individual concerned can material in these files be published.

The adoption of a comprehensive national law, however, could not quiet the debate over complicity and its influence. Although Havel asked for amendments to the national law to ensure further the right of individuals to appeal the results of the vetting, he revealed his own growing bitterness about the difficulties involved in rooting out Communist influence. For instance, after the passage of the screening law, Havel lamented:

> *Our revolution was carried out in the spirit of reconciliation, understanding, forgiveness, and repentance. All those involved in one way or another with the totalitarian system were given a magnanimous opportunity. They could leave their post quietly and inconspicuously. Nothing would have happened to them. They have not made use of this opportunity. They have just perked up. They have settled down in various new posts and positions and have even started to laugh at us.*

One deputy felt compelled to remind his colleagues that the point of screening is to prevent scandals over the long run, not to create them. Ideally, short-term discrediting would be compensated for by a government worthy of trust and respect over the long run.

An alternative view, however, holds that the undemocratic nature of the screening law itself will ultimately do more to damage the new democracy than the presence of former collaborators. As foreign minister Jiri Diestenbier argues:

> *Failure to respect the presumption of innocence, the introduction of the principle of collective guilt, the denial of legal counsel and the humiliation of a great number of honest people who made mistakes in the past but who hurt no one, is no way to move towards a law-abiding state.*

The view that screening constitutes unfair discrimination was recently echoed by the International Labor Organization. Due process concerns arise from the fact that only one small category of cases have the right to appeal the results of lustration and from the allegation that secret police records may be inaccurate or faked. Moreover, the law does not distinguish between motivations for informing or gradations of guilt parliament rejected an earlier version that called for sanctions only against those who could be proved to have "suppressed human rights." Those who carry out lustration have no leeway to pardon even those who signed only one record of interrogation and who never revealed anything damaging to others. Finally, lustration punishes "little informers" as much as, if not more than, their former bosses. One cartoon on this theme depicts a member of the Federal Assembly responding to the question of whether he is concerned about screening: "'Why worry? I was never recruited by the secret police; I was giving them orders.'"

The head of the interior ministry's commission in charge of appeals freely admits that legislation should be revised to address due process complaints. The law could, for instance, easily be changed to allow more appeals and to permit them before charges are disclosed. With regard to other complaints, examination of police procedure regarding informers reveals that, although the motivation and effects of informers are open to interpretation, a complicated filing and indexing system made creation of false records nearly impossible. Moreover, secret police periodically had to produce agents for inspection and often taped and filmed encounters;

invention of agents would have been difficult and would have brought about severe punishment if discovered. The vetting law was designed not to settle accounts but to cleanse public life; it seeks to avoid creation of a large unemployable pariah class by applying limited sanctions to a particular group of public servants. Lustration is confidential and carries no penalty besides ban from the offices named above.

There have been only three major attempts to subject former officials to criminal proceedings. The first concerned the use of force against demonstrators during the November revolution. The first secretary of the Prague branch of the Communist Party received a sentence of four years for ordering suppression of demonstrations, whereas a number of policemen received much shorter or suspended sentences for their roles in the November 17 incident. The former minister of the interior and his deputies were tried for the arbitrary detention of dissidents to block their participation in the demonstration. Their defense was that they were following the orders of the Communist Party's Central Committee. Other attempts to bring Communist leaders to justice have been less successful because of the twenty-year statute of limitations on most crimes. Thus, an indictment against the 1960s minister of the interior for crimes against detainees and prisoners was dismissed. Charges against twenty-two top party officials for treason for "inviting" Warsaw Pact troops into Czechoslovakia in 1968 also ran up against the statute of limitations barrier. Instead, charges were brought against the former prosecutor general, who failed to act on charges against these officials pressed by Charter 77 back in 1988, before the statute of limitations had expired. Thus, it appears that actual convictions of human rights abusers will be limited to the most recent years, when repression rarely took on a violent form.

Elsewhere in Eastern Europe

The same general questions of settling accounts encountered in Czechoslovakia arose in East Germany,

Poland, and Hungary, but in each case the treatment of the issues has varied. Let me simply note briefly that the GDR most resembles Czechoslovakia, not merely in the form of its transition to democracy but in the substance of its debates over coming to terms with the past. Here too, lack of pre election screening damaged the credibility of the new parliament. In terms of prosecutions, the East Germans, like the Czechoslovaks, have concentrated on recent events in this case, the fatal shootings of border crossers, aid to international terrorists, and corruption. Indeed, perhaps because of the myth of GDR economic superiority, East Germans have taken an enormous interest in economic "crimes" ranging from *nomenklatura* privileges to cases of outright embezzlement and fraud. The GDR's long-term resolution of issues of account settling are unique, however, because reunification has made possible the introduction of West German institutions and personnel to replace tainted East German counterparts. Despite charges of West German "colonization," the West German assumption of responsibility may defuse the potential instability caused by the process of settling accounts.

In Hungary and Poland, until 1992 the actual settling of accounts consisted largely of efforts to rehabilitate and compensate victims. Many Hungarians argue that the rarity of violence in recent years combined with the peacefulness of the transition make prosecutions unnecessary. Arguably, institutional change in Hungary is proceeding steadily with the aid of former Communists turned reformers. The slow pace of reform, however, produced a scandal when it came to light that the ministry of internal affairs had continued to spy on opposition parties after the latter had been legalized. Lustration has been raised by the radical opposition but more as a veiled threat than as a real possibility.

The issue of criminal prosecution of those involved in violently suppressing the 1956 uprising turned out to be extremely volatile. In 1991, the Hungarian legislature passed the "Zetenyi-Takacs Act," which declared that "the statute of limitations shall start again for the criminal offenses committed between December 21, 1944 and May 2, 1990 provided that the state's failure to prosecute said offenses was due to political reasons." The statute covered treason, torture resulting in death, and murder, which under Hungarian law is subject to a 20-year limitations period. Proponents of the law argued that because Communist Party control over prosecutors meant that high-ranking party officials were never prosecuted, the normal presumption that known criminals would be prosecuted within the statutory time period did not apply. The law was referred to the Constitutional Court for pre-enactment review, and the court found it unconstitutional. The initial decision held that a state based on the rule of law must have predictable and foreseeable laws, and that the "certainty of the law based on formal and objective principles is more important than necessarily partial and subjective justice."

Proponents of prosecutions then returned to the legislature. In March 1992, Parliament passed an authoritative resolution excluding the period between 1944 and 1989 from the operation of the statute of limitations, on grounds that the statute was tolled by the inability of the justice system to bring charges against Communist Party officials. This, too, the Constitutional Court struck down. Again in February 1993 the legislature sought to amend the law to force prosecutors to bring charges in the cases arising from the 1956 uprising, even if the trial itself would be barred by the statute of limitations. And again the Court rejected the bill.

Finally the legislature adopted a new approach, based on international law. The Act on Procedures Concerning Certain Crimes Committed During the 1956 Revolution permitted prosecutions for acts that violated the Geneva Conventions of 1949, especially Common Article 3 and Article 147 of the Fourth Convention defining grave breaches, as well as crimes against humanity as defined in article 6(c) of the Charter of the Nuremberg Tribunal. It then interpreted the killing of demonstrators and the torture and killing of political prisoners during the 1956 uprising to be war crimes and/or crimes against humanity under the Conventions or the Charter. These acts were not subject to statutes of limitations under the 1968 New York Convention on the Non-Applicability of Statutory Limitations to War Crimes and Crimes Against Humanity, which Hungary adopted in 1971.

The Constitutional Court upheld the law in October 1993. The Hungarian constitution provides that "the legal system of Hungary shall respect the universally accepted rules of international law, and shall ensure furthermore, the accord between the obligations assumed under international and domestic law." While the non-applicability of statutes of limitation to war crimes and crimes against humanity could not be considered part of international common law or universally accepted rules of international law, states that had ratified either the 1968 New York Convention or the similar 1974 European Convention assumed an obligation to prosecute according to the standards of international law. Moreover, the court held, "in this respect we are dealing with the development of international law in a clear direction, the process of which has not yet reached its final stage."

The court did not typify which acts qualified as war crimes and which as crimes against humanity. However, the judgment stressed that, unlike the more narrowly drawn "grave breaches" provisions, the obligations of Common Article 3 of the Geneva Conventions, applicable in non-international conflicts, are minimal requirements that conflicting parties must apply "always and under all circumstances." They are based on elementary considerations of humanity and cannot be violated in any armed conflict.

Since October 1993, at least a dozen people have been arrested, accused of taking part in mass shootings of unarmed civilians in 1956. Veterans groups as well as the

Justice Ministry have been compiling documents from 1956. It remains to be seen, however, whether prosecutions can weather both changes in the ruling coalition and the evidentiary difficulties involved.

Poland also moved slowly to confront former human rights abusers. This reluctance to settle accounts actively apparently also stems from the compromise transition process. Walesa defends Poland's negotiated "35 percent democracy" by arguing:

> *We have done everything very prudently, and we have not even antagonized the Communist Party members too much. This will bring us advantages. Accounts will be settled with the old regime but this should not be our main goal. However, I fear that Europe expects us to settle accounts drastically.*

Hesitancy regarding radical political reform allowed the Polish secret police and military security forces to destroy hundreds of thousands of incriminating documents. Moreover, by 1991 Poland's parliamentary commission investigating over 100 mysterious deaths under the old regime had still received little help from the Communist-controlled ministry of internal affairs. In June 1992, a divided parliament finally addressed the subject of lustration, with disastrous results. Having learned that the new minister of internal affairs was preparing an investigation of secret police files on the urging of a more radical prime minister, the Sjem demanded immediate disclosure, despite the fact that the investigation was incomplete and had been hastily and sloppily conducted. The list given to parliament included all of the deputies listed in secret police registers regardless of whether they were agents or objects of surveillance. In the resulting furor, parliament voted the government out of power for having favored lustration. Given the inaccuracies of the first attempt at lustration, anger turned against its instigators and executors and no one named as a collaborator resigned from parliament. The question now is whether to make a second effort at lustration to clear up the confusion sowed by the first.

Lessons from East Central Europe

Although few Communist regimes remain to be overthrown, the experience of post Communist governments in East Central Europe holds several potentially valuable lessons for transitions from repressive rule. Paradoxically, both Walesa and Havel thought they had successfully negotiated a path to democracy when they avoided a Communist backlash; instead, they encountered an unforeseen anti-Communist backlash. The spectacle of Communist officials and functionaries continuing to profit and dominate through their economic and political posts gradually aroused popular embarrassment and resentment. Even Hungary and Poland where the very process of transition by compromise instilled some patience for gradual change and blurred the distinction between "bad" Communists and "good" alliance partners -faced pressure to implement greater "justice." Disillusionment with pacts grew over time, spurted by the realization that the "late developers" East Germany and Czechoslovakia had surpassed Poland and Hungary in the extent and speed of reform.

The speed and nonviolence of the civic revolutions in Czechoslovakia and the GDR, on the other hand, unrealistically heightened public expectations of radical change in personnel and institutions. As Havel has reluctantly concluded, the mistake was [not] made immediately in the first revolutionary days, when we allegedly were too tactful toward the adversary. Those who claim this have forgotten too soon the fact that the previous regime had at its disposal, to the last minute various power instruments. The mistake was perhaps made a bit later, in the first months of 1990, when we all underestimated the exceptional artfulness of our former adversaries.

Ultimately, the debate over purging collaborators seems inescapable because the former Communist nomenklatura has neither transformed itself nor been unseated by modesty or market mechanisms. Even economic pragmatism has not provided a durable rationale for ignoring the abuses of the past in post communist states as elites incompatible with the new regime remain entrenched in the economy as well as in government, and indeed over time have managed to win elections in several countries.

In practical terms, because the democrats feel "we are not like them," the new rulers have been frustrated by their inability quickly and fairly to unseat the old apparat. As pointed out earlier, collaboration does not lend itself to legal prosecution. Indeed, unlike Latin American transitions where human rights abusers could be clearly targeted for prosecution, the vast majority of former East European officials rest secure in the knowledge of having technically committed no crimes. This sense of impunity contributes to their reluctance to withdraw from public life after all, unlike military rulers, they have no "barracks" to which to return. Many feel that compensation to victims is not enough to restore justice and prevent a return to repression. In Czechoslovakia lustration served as a compromise between "forgiveness" and "prosecution."

Advocates of lustration argue that the presence of former secret police agents and collaborators in high posts could be a potential time bomb: Not only might such people be open to blackmail but they also arguably lack the appropriate character for public service. On the other hand, opponents note that all who lived under communism carry some guilt, some complicity, for the maintenance of an oppressive system. They contend that the government's authority and dignity might be undermined more by controversies and scandals over the past than by the presence of a few former collaborators. Some opponents even argue that lustration means a "belated victory" for the secret police because police records provided the grounds for "certificates of moral hygiene."

If one concludes that allowing the immense secret police network of informers to exist untouched breeds a suspicion that undermines new democracies, the evidence from East Central Europe indicates that the method of lustration matters a great deal. Looking at the shortcomings of the Czechoslovak experience, one sees, for instance, that pre election screening of candidates, by giving parties a chance to submit lists to be checked against secret police records, can prevent unnecessary scandals. In terms of screening and punishment, evenhandedness toward collaborators is important, even if "justice" is elusive. This means formulating and enforcing a comprehensive screening law from the beginning rather than relying on ad hoc dismissals. Lustration on a case-by-case basis is open to political manipulation and offers no mechanism for victims of rumor to clear themselves. The Czechoslovak attempt to formalize lustration uncovered further potential pitfalls. It allowed lustration to far overreach legislators' original intentions because whereas it mandated lustration for certain posts, the law did not preclude screening of others so that school cooks, among others, are now subject to vetting. Moreover, lack of a strong appeals system in the administrative screening process created due process problems. A judicial mechanism might better protect individual rights and could allow the flexibility necessary for evaluation of mitigating circumstances.

9

Legal Setting for Human Rights

Introduction

It is now 1994, and the number of countries slowly and painfully coming to terms with their governments' past treatment of its citizens has grown. In Chile, the elected regime has moved to investigate violations and compensate victims but not in most cases to prosecute. In the former USSR and in several Eastern European countries the accountability of the prior regimes and methods of redress for their victims are urgent matters of public discussion. In South Africa, Cambodia, Haiti, El Salvador, and Guatemala, questions of investigation, accountability, and redress have been a major factor in negotiations toward domestic or internationally sponsored transitions, even as human rights abuses often continue. And in those countries that have confronted questions of impunity in the recent past Argentina and Uruguay, for example it is now possible to attempt an evaluation.

As the transitional regimes emerge, they inherit a legacy of widespread repression against the civilian population. In some cases, this repression has taken the form of massive killings of real or perceived political opponents; in others, opponents were forcibly kidnapped and disappeared; in still others, citizens were tortured and imprisoned; and elsewhere, selective killings combined with imprisonment were the norm. In each case, the official or quasi-official status of the perpetrators shielded them from sanction, creating a culture of impunity in which the most inhumane acts could be carried out without fear of repercussions.

In some of the cases studied, these actors have wrestled with whether, and to what extent, a government should engage in official investigations of prior wrongdoing by state officials. They have had to determine whether some, or most, of those responsible for the worst crimes should be brought to justice, even if this means annulling a previous amnesty law or risking a violent backlash by military or security forces. Finally, they have had to decide whether and how to compensate the victims of the prior regime. Where the shape of the future government or its commitment to human rights is still being negotiated, the parties to the negotiation must decide how much to insist on and how much to concede. And in still other countries, notably those of Eastern Europe, the question is not only one of risk to the new regime from a disgruntled party or military class but of the breadth of collaboration with the former regimes and the means for distinguishing the more from the less culpable.

Any transition from authoritarian rule to greater democracy necessarily involves efforts to establish and promote the rule of law. Societies in which massive human rights violations occur with impunity are by definition lawless societies. The lawlessness of the state itself serves to disempower ordinary citizens, making them fearful to think or speak out and breeding cynicism and passivity. As societies attempt to recover from these periods of lawlessness, one of the first opportunities to reestablish the primacy of law over individuals comes in the treatment of the former rulers, torturers, and jailers. If such people are treated summarily, extracting an eye for an eye, the transition to a society of laws is set back immeasurably. On the other hand, a blanket amnesty and silence from the new government perpetuate the existence of a separate class to whom the rule of law does not apply. Continued impunity equally undermines efforts to reestablish legality. Thus, the need to define legal procedures and criteria for dealing with past abuses takes on a special importance. Similarly, the mechanisms devised to settle accounts with those responsible for such abuses must meet certain criteria for fairness and predictability that are traditionally the province of law. Finally, much of the fight over impunity has been waged in terms of trials, domestic legislation, and international legal responsibilities. As a result, much of this book is written by and for lawyers.

At the same time, however, law is never made in a vacuum. It is always part of a larger political, moral, and social dynamic. Thus, the book is not exclusively about law or for lawyers. It includes the insights and efforts of political and social scientists, historians, and journalists, as well as human rights experts who combine the skills of several disciplines.

As governmental and nongovernmental actors frame the legal and policy debate, they look to the experiences of other countries. To design a strategy for dealing with their own past, actors learn from what has been successful or unsuccessful elsewhere.

Discussion of how to deal with past human rights violations in law as well as in politics and morality takes place on two levels. First, national societies debate the effects of pursuing official investigations, prosecutions or civil penalties, or compensation mechanisms. The extent and severity of past violations, the prior history of democratic rule in the country, the number of victims, the extent of complicity by the citizenry, cultural and historical traditions, the stability of the new government, and the press of other especially economic matters provide a unique context in each case. So too do the character of the liberalization (top down or bottom up), the strength of civil society, especially human rights or victims' groups, and the amount of time elapsed between the acts at issue and the transition or liberalization.

These debates raise the fundamental question of the appropriate decision makers in a given society. Are these decisions that should be made by government officials as part of their routine tasks, or are they so fundamental to a nation's self definition that they should be subject to some specific mechanism for public choice? What if, as many argue was the case in Uruguay, for example, public approval mechanisms are subject to inordinate pressures from those who benefit from impunity? And even more basic, if the victims of repression constitute a discreet minority, isn't there a danger that majoritarian decision making will trample on whatever rights to redress victims may have in a morally unacceptable fashion? Or put differently, if we are talking about rights to redress, doesn't the right to demand justice or to forgive belong only to those directly harmed and not to the polity as a whole? Or is the harm against the whole society, both past and potential future victims alike? It is the resonance of these profound moral issues that makes the issue of impunity so complex and evocative of impassioned debate.

On a second level, the legal, political, and moral choices involved are to some degree shaped by the requirements of the international community. International law especially shapes limits to what national governments can openly do and establishes minimum requirements for compliance. As I hope to show, international law provides considerable guidance on issues of investigation, prosecution, and compensation, although admittedly its relevance has not always been recognized.

In formulating policies for dealing with past violations of fundamental rights, international law can be an important source of support for transitional regimes. If international law mandates investigation, prosecution, and redress, for example, the new government must somehow find ways to comply or else suffer real costs in terms of international isolation, opprobrium, or loss of trade or aid. These costs take the decision to comply with the law out of the realm of the merely possible, and therefore negotiable, and place it in the realm of the mandatory and nonnegotiable. For a weak transitional regime facing powerful constraints, a perceived lack of bargaining power on this point may be a boon. As a corollary, a decision to investigate or prosecute mandated by international law is less likely to be seen as political capitulation to a given faction or group or as mere vengeance.

Furthermore, reference to international law is mandated by the nature of the human rights violations at issue. In most of the cases studied in this book, past regimes engaged in a massive, systematic pattern of arbitrary killings, torture, and/or forced disappearances. These acts are clearly prohibited under international law. Moreover, they constitute a small subset of violations of physical integrity, which historically have been subject to the highest possible degree of protection. Whereas other types of human rights have been the subject of controversy, there is widespread agreement among both states and scholars that rights to physical integrity merit special protection. Such rights are nonderogable even in times of war or national emergency; the norms protecting them are widely considered peremptory norms; and the perpetrators are subject to universal jurisdiction. There is a widely shared moral sense that such violations of physical integrity are affronts to human dignity on the most basic level. Thus, although it is possible that other types of human rights violations might merit similar treatment.

State-initiated and condoned killings, torture, and disappearances violate specific rights defined in widely subscribed instruments, including the Universal

Declaration of Human Rights, the International Covenant on Civil and Political Rights, the American Convention on Human Rights, and the European Convention for the Protection of Human Rights and Fundamental Freedoms. Specific treaties concerning torture and disappearances, resolutions of U.N. bodies, and court cases establishing torture and disappearance as violations of customary law all point to the clear international prohibition on states' killing, torturing, or forcibly causing the disappearance of their own citizens.

Treaty-based obligations give all other states parties to the treaty the right to scrutinize one another's performance and to demand compliance. To the extent the treaties involved contain individual complaint mechanisms, individuals and organizations as well as states may raise treaty violations. And to the extent the rights not to be subjected to torture, summary execution, or disappearance emanate from customary law, they give rise to obligations owed by each state to the international community as a whole. These obligations also underlie the relevance of international law to the topic at hand.

In many countries, most notably in Latin America but also in South Africa, the Philippines, and others, the nature of these human rights violations has changed as governments have developed novel forms of repression. Most important are the related techniques of forced disappearance and use of paramilitary forces to carry out repressive activities. The emergence of these methods as preferred instruments of dictatorship provides yet another reason why the debate over impunity both concerns and can benefit from the perspectives of international law.

There are two main elements of a forced disappearance: first, "abduction or detention by an agent of a State or by a person acting with the consent or acquiescence of a State" and, second, official refusal to acknowledge the abduction or to disclose information that would reveal the detainee's fate. Those who are abducted are typically detained, tortured, and eventually killed. A death squad killing similarly involves state involvement or complicity and a denial of responsibility but differs in that the body, usually mutilated and tortured, is deliberately left where it can be found. In either case, the techniques serve to terrorize broad sectors of the population, leaving the families and friends of those who have disappeared in permanent anguish and chilling political and social activity. The overall effect of years of inexplicable disappearances and of the horror of mutilated corpses appearing at roadsides is to create a psychologically cowed population, where people retreat into themselves and into denial of their own and others' rights as a matter of self-preservation.

The use of disappearances and death squads rather than outright arrest or official execution allows the regime to deny all accountability. The government can rid itself of actual, potential, or perceived opponents without the publicity of a public trial or the risk of creating martyrs; and through disguising and denying its responsibility it can make it difficult for citizens to press for either formal trial or release of detainees. These techniques leave little credible and specific evidence of official involvement. In the Argentine case, for instance, Orders were given orally in most cases, requiring the cooperative testimony of junior officers who are constitutionally entitled to the right against self-incrimination. Written orders were either unsigned or couched so vaguely as to communicate their true intent only by "subliminal intimation." Official statements during military rule denied any illegality. Kidnappers drove unmarked cars; torturers wore no uniforms and employed pseudonyms; victims were kept blindfolded; detention centers were often established on private rather than public property.

Similarly, on an international level, the government may deny all responsibility and take refuge in the refrain that it is "investigating these lamentable occurrences." The strong international and domestic prohibitions on arbitrary execution, torture, and disappearances lose their effectiveness if governments may simply stonewall and delay, insisting that the burden of proof is on their victims to show official involvement. To make these prohibitions meaningful, law must respond by placing affirmative obligations on governments obligations that include investigating, prosecuting, and compensating.

Whether or not these obligations are compelled by effective law, the question remains whether they are sound policy. The arguments for and against investigation, prosecution, and compensation are similar, although some questions are specific to each.

The debate over investigation turns on differing perceptions of the best way to prevent future abuses. Proponents of investigation argue that a society which moves forward without confronting its past is condemned to repeat it. Investigation draws a clear line between past and future, allowing the beginning of a healing process. During a period of repression, vast sectors of society will have closed themselves off from an inhospitable political world, choosing not to see the violence around them or justifying it on the grounds that the victims must have done something wrong to deserve their fate. Investigation reveals the extent of repression and the degree to which the victims were valuable members of the society (or merely random targets). Although such an investigation may be carried out by nongovernment groups, an official imprimatur lends authority and a recognition that these were state-sanctioned abuses. The difference between unofficial and official recognition has been described as "the difference between knowledge and acknowledgement. It's what happens and can only happen to knowledge when it is made part of the public cognitive scene." Investigation becomes a kind of unofficial apology, giving official voice and legitimacy to those who spoke up during the years of repression and were dissmissed as subversives, crazies, or dissidents.

As a form of redress, investigation also allows victims and especially their families to put the past to rest. In cases of forced disappearance, this is crucial because the victims' fate may be unknown, and families may pass anguished years believing their loved one is alive in some clandestine prison. In any case, investigation of the fate of the victims, publication of their names, and recognition of the fact that they were wronged rescues them from oblivion if not from death, at least in a symbolic sense. In a broader sense, too, investigation is part of a struggle for the control of history. It plays a central role in a society's redefinition of itself. By discrediting the official version of the former dictatorship's actions, it does not allow that version of history to be perpetuated in the military academies or in textbooks. "Dirty wars" may no longer be excused in the name of fighting communism, maintaining a way of life, or defending the proletarian state.

Opponents of official investigations have argued that such investigations may do more harm than good. By dwelling on the past, they argue, a deeply divided society will be unable to overcome its divisions and move forward. Old hatreds and vengeances will be dredged up and replayed ad infinitum, yet the overriding need is to let bygones be bygones and move forward in a spirit of conciliation. Furthermore, there are practical difficulties in investigations: How much proof of government involvement should investigations require? Should the names of the alleged perpetrators be made public as a form of social punishment when no other sanction seems forthcoming, or should no one be publicly accused without the chance to clear his or her name before a court of law? How broad should the inquiry sweep? Should it cover only government wrongs or also those of government opponents, especially armed opponents?

Prosecutions raise a related set of concerns. Proponents argue that prosecutions represent an efficient way of ascertaining the truth; the legal process ensures that fact finding will be thorough and reasonably impartial and will lead to a clear declaration of fault. In addition, prosecutions will punish or at least stigmatize the guilty, deter potential lawbreakers, and provide a warning that future transgressions will not be excused. More generally, prosecutions may be useful for reestablishing the rule of law, underlining the discontinuity between the new government and the old, and reinforcing the primacy of civilian institutions in the new order. Moreover, a failure to prosecute may well embolden the military or security forces or other remnants of the old regime, making it harder for civilian control to take root. The culture of impunity will continue unless the cycle is broken.

From the point of view of the victims, prosecutions channel the desire for private vengeance while "restoring citizens to full membership in society by suppressing the differences between those who had control over other persons' lives and those whose existence was at their mercy." For the population in general, prosecutions help restore citizens' dignity after years of defenselessness based on state terror.

The main argument specifically against prosecutions is that they may destabilize a still-fragile transitional government past the breaking point. Thus, moving to punish violators may result in prolonged political instability or even a return of dictatorship. Furthermore, prosecutions hastily organized by a transitional state may be used as a cover for personal, political, tribal, or localized grievances, with the state unable to differentiate sufficiently between meritorious and spurious complaints. The promise of prosecutions may deter some dictators from abandoning power. Finally, opponents argue, overwhelming practical obstacles exist to prosecuting all those responsible for grave violations of physical integrity during periods of generalized repression. The courts will be clogged, and evidence will be difficult or impossible to collect if large groups or institutions are complicit. The authority of the civilian government will be undermined if it decides to press forward, only to find itself unable to subject the former rulers or torturers to legal process.

In the case of the military, difficult questions of how far up or down the ranks to prosecute must be answered. In part, these questions reflect the legal status in national and international law of the defense of superior orders; but in part they also reflect the practical problems of keeping a tightly knit institution from closing ranks and of devising incentive structures that facilitate cooperation. The fear is that deadlock will result, squandering society's material and political resources rather than building preventive rules and institutions for the future.

Several more thorny questions arise in the prosecution context. For instance, are the possibilities for state action limited to penal sanctions, or should we widen our views to include other state-imposed sanctions, including loss of pension, loss of military rank, inability to hold public office, or others? If convicted, must extorturers or dictators serve their full sentences, or is a pardon permissible? If the latter, must they serve jail time at all? Is there some proportionality requirement in either domestic law or morality or in international law requiring the punishment to fit the crime? If so, is that requirement affected by the need to obtain eyewitnesses or other traditional prosecutorial concerns?

In addition to investigation and prosecution, transitional governments may attempt to confront a legacy of past violations by directly or indirectly compensating the victims. Compensation may be in the form of monetary payments (either from government or through civil suits) or it may be symbolic, ranging from public reburial to official apologies to monuments to a general fund in the victims' name dedicated to preventing future violations. In any case, proponents argue, compensation, although it clearly cannot bring back the victims' life or health, expresses in tangible form a societal recognition of wrongfulness. To the extent a compensation program honors the memory of the victims, its effects are similar to investigation. To the extent that monetary payments from either the perpetrator or state institutions serve a deterrent function, they parallel both investigation and prosecution.

Although compensation programs seem to be less controversial than either investigation or prosecution, more questions arise. For example, in countries in which most of the population has suffered under a past government, widespread compensation may be neither financially feasible nor morally justifiable. How can a society draw lines between those who suffered earlier or later or more or less? Second, should the compensation be paid from a general taxpayers' fund, or is it possible to target the budgets of those institutions (say, the military) most directly responsible? Third, should victims always be treated as individuals, or is there a role for collective compensation to discrete groups? Finally, there is a risk that requiring survivors and their families to come forward publicly and claim compensation may in itself be traumatic, rekindling old fears.

The rest of this book explores these dilemmas in law and politics. Part I establishes a general framework in the law. After a brief introductory look at why societies choose to provide redress to those harmed and to punish the harm-doer, it focuses on the international law limits and obligations of states with respect to investigation, prosecution, and compensation. It looks first at rules that may be found in international treaties, and then at those that arise from customary law or general principles of law. It then focuses on some of the knottier legal problems in the area, including the legality of amnesties, superior orders, and statute of limitations concerns.

The studies focus on national experiences with issues of investigation, prosecution, and compensation for grave human rights violations during the 1980s and 1990s. They look at the difficulties, dilemmas, and lessons learned in each national experience, and explore the role of international law and the international community in addressing these issues. They include societies in which a military dictatorship or pervasive party and security apparatus was replaced by a civilian regime that promised more openness and democracy, and those in which national and, increasingly, international negotiations to end a civil conflict include as a prominent component the question of the abuses of the prior regime. Each part begins with an introductory overview chapter which both situates the subsequent chapters in historical context and allows for brief discussion of other relevant experiences from the region.

Finally, the last chapter, Conclusion: Combatting Impunity, seeks to distill the experiences recounted and analyzed in the country chapters, in light of the legal obligations established in the legal chapters, into more general conclusions. This chapter examines what has worked, what has not, and what lessons the experiences to date hold for the future. I also consider the role of law, especially international law, in defining parameters and standards for action. Finally, I suggest ways to make the law on impunity more precise and responsive within a framework that includes both national and international approaches.

10

Human Rights in Haiti: Searching for Peace

Introduction

It remains unclear, however, whether the international efforts will again founder on the intransigence of the most powerful forces in Haiti the economic elite and the military and paramilitary forces. Even assuming that these corporative forces can be brought under democratic control, the difficulties of creating a viable economy, an institutional structure, and respect for the rule of law, which must undergird both, remain formidable. The question of whether to prosecute those who have committed serious human rights violations played a key role in the events leading up to the September 1991 coup. That question continued to be significant in negotiations for President Jean-Bertrand Aristide's return and is now a key question in the consolidation of the democratic government. Indeed, dealing with the past will be crucial to opening up new possibilities for establishing the rule of law in both the institutions and the minds of the Haitian people.

The Origins of Dictatorship

The history of Haiti is a tragic tale of political corruption and military violence. With the singular exception of one regime that governed between 1818 and 1843, Haiti has been marked by ceaseless coups, assassinations, and massive violations of human rights. The only period of relative stability was between 1915 and 1934 when the U.S. Marines occupied the country in order to ensure U.S. commercial privileges. When the troops were finally removed, conventional hostilities with the Dominican Republic resumed.

Any notion of stability from that point meant dictatorship. First, it was the regime of François (Papa Doc) Duvalier, who ruled with an iron fist between 1957 and his death in 1971 with the aid of a maniacal private security force known as the Tonton Macoutes. Papa Doc consolidated his power quickly and ruthlessly, eviscerating individual liberties and political opposition with equal dispatch. Indeed, over 40,000 Haitians reportedly lost their lives as the victims of official brutality. Duvalier stole over $500 million in foreign aid and taxes and deposited the money into personal accounts in Haiti and abroad. Officials at all levels of government, taking their cue from Duvalier, took part in similar acts of corruption.

Papa Doc remained in power for over fourteen years, and in order to ensure a legacy of Duvalier control over the country, organized a referendum on January 31, 1971, in which voters approved his nineteen-year-old son, Jean-Claude (Baby Doc), as his successor. When his father died, Jean-Claude became "President for Life." His rule was as repressive as his father's. In 1986, however, when the levels of economic disparities and political corruption reached ungovernable proportions, Baby Doc fled Haiti for exile in France.

Following the Duvaliers came a series of political regimes that owed their survival to a large military caste which operated with the indefatigable support of a small upper class. None of these regimes, however, had the support of the Haitian people. Each ruled through the power of the gun.

Nonetheless, the fall of the Duvaliers raised expectations that some of the military and security forces, including the Duvalier-associated Tonton Macoutes, would be brought to justice. In the weeks after Duvalier was ousted, mobs killed a number of known Macoutes. After crowds looted the home of former secret police chief Luc Desir and prevented him from leaving the country, the Namphy government promised to arrest and bring to justice the persons suspected of committing serious crimes during the twenty-eight years of Duvalier rule. Spurred by large demonstrations demanding justice, the government did prosecute several lowranking Army officers, and three Macoutes were tried and convicted of killing political prisoners. However, the regime also allowed a number of high-ranking officers, including the head of the Macoutes and the former Army intelligence chief, to leave the country; others known to have committed crimes were freed after Army courts found insufficient evidence to convict them. According to human rights activists, intimidation of witnesses and jurors made bringing such cases to trial extremely difficult. Whatever small advances were made initially soon became buried under a new wave of Army shootings, repeated coups, and instability.

The popular will was finally expressed in 1990. The Haitian people elected Jean-Bertrand Aristide to the office of president in December 1990 in the first fully democratic election to take place in Haiti in nearly 200 years. Popular support for Aristide was astonishing: He received two thirds of the vote, giving him an unprecedented mandate for reform.

Equally impressive was the election process. It represented the culmination of an extraordinary international effort to launch Haiti on the path to democracy. Both the Organization of American States (OAS) and the United Nations actively participated in helping Haitian officials assure the security and dignity of the election process. Voter turnout was remarkably high; 75 percent of the eligible voters approximately 2.7 million out of the 3.2 million registered voters turned out to vote despite extremely difficult logistical problems. The dirt roads and mountain paths of rural Haiti, where three quarters of the population lives, made the distribution of election materials particularly hazardous. Moreover, the high illiteracy rate of Haitians compounded the challenge of registering and voting. Nevertheless, despite these problems, virtually all observers who monitored the voting claimed that the elections were fair and that voters experienced no intimidation. In addition, the military helped assure that violence would not occur.

This peaceful, positive election, however, soon gave way to violence. Even before Aristide took his oath of office, the military challenged his legitimacy in an unsuccessful coup, and coup attempts continued throughout his tenure. The September 1991 coup was not only successful but it has also resulted in a widely publicized reign of terror in Haiti.

During its short tenure, the Aristide government took important steps to improve the rule of law in Haiti. In one of his first official acts, President Aristide announced the retirement of senior military officials who had either been involved in past human rights violations or had failed to punish persons responsible for such abuses. He also appointed several new public prosecutors and removed corrupt officials linked to the military. Simultaneously, Aristide announced the creation of a human rights commission charged with investigating some of the most notorious human rights abuses that had been committed in the past. The new president also closed down Fort Dimanche, known as a torture center, and dedicated a museum to its victims on the site. In addition, under the Aristide government, a number of people believed to have been involved in a 1987 massacre were arrested, as were others alleged to have directed killings and torture under past regimes. Unfortunately, Aristide was overthrown before these individuals could come to trial.

The most significant step Aristide took to improve respect for the rule of law was the dissolution of the institution of rural section chiefs who were accountable solely to the military authorities. These section chiefs had unfettered control over the lives of the peasants in rural areas. This unchecked power led to systematic disregard of human rights with complete impunity. The Aristide government replaced the section chiefs' system with a system of rural police under the jurisdiction of the ministry of justice. It appointed a completely new corps of rural agents made up of individuals untainted by the abuses of the old system.

But these reforms did not last long. The overthrow of the Aristide government has resulted in the deaths and torture of thousands of innocent people that continues to the present day. Moreover, after the overthrow of Aristide, the military rapidly took steps to consolidate power. It named a civilian government, including an interim president, to complicate the return of President Aristide. It reversed the systemic changes made by the Aristide government. First, the military fired or hunted down many of the prosecution and judicial officials who had been appointed by Aristide. Next, it released prisoners, including Tonton Macoutes, who had been convicted of human rights violations during Aristide's presidency. The military also restored the old section chief structure, thus returning to power individuals who were known to have committed massive human rights abuses. These section chiefs, in turn, enlisted their old private armies, formerly known as the Tonton Macoutes but now referred to as attachés, and reasserted their control over the countryside.

International Efforts to Restore Aristide to the Presidency

Over the next two years the international community made serious efforts to help restore Aristide to power and to support the nascent democratic movement in Haiti. The diplomatic reaction of the OAS and the United Nations was vigorous and forceful. The member states of the OAS froze the assets of Haiti and imposed a trade embargo on the country. There followed a round of negotiations, under U.N. and OAS auspices, that stretched out over the next year and a half. By April 1993, the outlines of a settlement were visible. The sticking point turned out to be amnesty for the past human rights violations of the military.

As part of the price for Aristide's reinstatement, the military demanded a complete amnesty. In February 1993, Aristide agreed to a general amnesty for political crimes but refused to extend the amnesty to "common criminals." He argued that the Haitian Constitution forbade such an amnesty, adding that he believed the killings and torture by Army leaders would subject the latter to prosecution as common criminals. Intense negotiations took place in March and April. The U.S. and U.N. negotiators made no secret of their belief that a full amnesty was necessary and that Aristide was being unrealistic as well as intransigent. Aristide supporters, for their part, accused the United Nations and the U.S. administration of exerting enormous pressure on Aristide to accept an illegal amnesty, thus making the cost of a settlement prohibitively high in order to blame the exiled president if the talks collapsed. Finally, Aristide apparently gave in to the increasing pressure to settle, agreeing to guarantee freedom from criminal prosecutions and not to oppose future parliamentary efforts to preclude civil suits against the military. In exchange, the settlement was to include creation of a "Truth Commission" to investigate the most serious abuses. The military rejected this deal, however, and, as a result, the international community imposed stricter sanctions, including an oil embargo.

The culmination of these negotiations was the July 1993 Governors Island Agreement. Under this agreement, President Aristide agreed to appoint a prime minister who would be subject to confirmation by parliament, after which the embargo would be suspended. The agreement further provided that the U.N. and OAS sanctions would be suspended at the initiative of the respective secretaries general of the two organizations immediately after the new prime minister "is confirmed and assumes office." President Aristide would return to Haiti on October 30, 1993. Shortly before his return, Cédras would retire from the high command in favor of an Aristide appointee, who would then name new members to the high command "in accordance with the constitution." Other coup participants would be allowed to remain in the military, but they would be posted outside Haiti. The agreement also gave Aristide the right to appoint a new chief of police to head a reorganized police force for Port-au-Prince, which would no longer be part of the military. An international police force would be stationed in Haiti, and other steps would be taken to "modernize" the Army. Moreover, in connection with the agreement, an international aid program amounting to $1 billion over five years would be instituted. Finally, there would be international cooperation in matters of technical and financial development aid and assistance for administrative and judicial reform.

The Governors Island Agreement provided for full amnesty granted by the president to the coup leaders and supporters within the framework of article 147 of the national constitution and "implementation of other instruments which may be adopted by the Parliament." Article 147 allows a presidential amnesty only for political matters "as stipulated by law." Thus, if parliament defines the military's human rights violations as "political," they would be covered by the amnesty. Violence and intimidation and the total abrogation of the Governors Island Agreement by the military kept Parliament from meeting to define the issue, although Aristide's government at one point agreed to the amnesty.

The Governors Island Agreement was a total failure. Neither Cedras nor François resigned. Instead, Cedras broke every part of the brokered deal and employed every kind of delay while subordinates known as attachés continued to terrorize the population. Their terror knew no bounds. They assassinated the largest financial backer of Aristide, Antoine Izmery, pulling him from a church in broad daylight and shooting him in the streets. They also assassinated the minister of justice, Guy Malary. The Haitians who could, fled the capital, hoping the countryside would be safer. Like the attachés, the men at the top appeared determined not to lose the power they amassed since the coup. Indeed, they made huge amounts of money from control of the ports and taxation, and some shared in the drug trade that moved through Haiti at a rapid Clip.

When Cedras reneged on the agreement, the United Nations imposed a new embargo on oil and arms shipments, and U.S. and allied warships encircled the nation. The new sanctions included freezing all assets in the United States owned by Haitians residing in their homeland. The freezing of these assets represented the Clinton administration's attempt to show the powerful Haitian elite that they would not be allowed to escape the consequences of their support for an illegitimate and illegal government. The U.N. sanctions also called for a total trade embargo. The immediate and most significant result of the embargo was the discontinuation of all commercial air travel to and from Haiti. The freeze and the embargo, however, did not result in the removal of the military coup leaders. The effectiveness of the sanctions was weakened by the almost free flow of contraband goods, especially gasoline, across the Dominican Republic border. Only under significant U.S. pressure did Joaquin Balaguer, President of the Dominican Republic, agree to take steps to enforce the international embargo.

Although sanctions hurt, they may not have been enough without a credible threat of force. Though impoverished Haitians suffered severe deprivation under an on-again, off-again embargo, the military bosses prospered from rising prices and trade in smuggled goods. While the latest embargo eventually pushed Cedras toward another negotiation, it was not likely to destroy the power of the military. So how was the United States and the international community to fulfill its pledge not just to restore President Aristide to office but also to ensure the growth of a lasting democratic nation?

The United States, of course, was particularly concerned with this question. As of now, there is only one way Haiti makes its problems matter in the United States (or elsewhere internationally, for that matter) by having thousands of desperate asylum-seeking refugees attempt the hazardous 600-mile journey by sea to Miami. Indeed, Haitian boat people are a large concern to President Clinton, who until very recently continued the Bush policy of returning the boat people to Haiti without hearings on their asylum claims, in flagrant violation of international law.

The Clinton administration, under intense political pressure from many members of Congress, especially the Congressional Black Caucus, and human rights groups, changed its policy of forcibly returning Haitians stopped at sea. Instead, the administration agreed to hold interviews on board vessels docked at third countries and to take those Haitians found to have a well-founded fear of persecution to the United States for further processing of their asylum claims.

Because of this change in policy and increased acts of violence against the Haitian people by the Haitian military, thousands of Haitians fled Haiti in boats. In response to this newest flood of refugees, President Clinton changed his policy once again. Instead of allowing those refugees with a well-founded fear of persecution to come to the United States for processing, his latest policy required sending those Haitians to third countries. As exemplified by the Clinton administration's vacillating Haitian refugee policy, as well as the United States and international communities' shifting policy toward Haiti during the past century, establishing a functioning democracy in Haiti may, over the long term, not maintain the support of the international community.

At the same time, the United Nations gave the Clinton administration its backing for the use of force in Haiti. On July 31, 1994, the Security Council, by a 12to-zero vote, authorized a U.S. invasion and occupation of Haiti if the international sanctions and embargo failed to remove the illegitimate military regime. After this chapter was completed, and as this book was going to press, U.S. troops entered Haiti pursuant to a last-minute deal between the U.S. government and Haiti's military leaders. While the full outlines are not yet known, the deal called for Cédras and François to leave their posts (although not necessarily the country) by October 15, 1994 or the date the Haitian Parliament passed a sweeping amnesty law, whichever came first. U.S. troops were to ensure that the deal went through as well as help retrain the Army and the police; the current military structure was to remain intact. The embargo was to be lifted immediately. President Aristide and his advisers, however, questioned the ability of the accord to protect Aristide supporters while the military still retained full power. In addition, according to press reports, Aristide expressed opposition to the amnesty provisions of the deal, which provide not only amnesty for political crimes but also for murder, rape, and other crimes committed by military and security forces from 1991 on. Aristide pointed out that the "notion that crimes against humanity, murders and tortures can be amnestied by Parliament" would "contradict the Haitian Constitution."

While an invasion may solve the immediate problem by removing the military leaders, it does not solve the more difficult task of creating the conditions for a viable democracy to flourish in Haiti. Indeed, the last time the Marines invaded Haiti, in 1915, they stayed for almost two decades and achieved very little in the way of building a democratic nation. Haiti has never had a secure democratic government, and it is not clear that there are enough functioning elements of civil society left to provide a proper foundation for such a government within the period of time the U.S. public and the international community will support an international presence. The successors of Cedras and François are still present, and the country is still split between a tiny elite and a vast poor majority. What, if any, alternatives exist? The answer begins with a focus on the complex issues involved in any transition to democracy, especially one that may take place in Haiti.

Institutions, Imagination, and the Rule of Law

Several thorny and intertwined problems in Haiti's movement toward democracy must be resolved if the transition is to succeed without causing great harm to masses of people. Institutional structures must be developed and secured. Economic and political stability must be assured. Corporatist social and political structures must be transformed so that the powerless receive their fair share of the basic necessities of life. The rule of law must become paramount in the formal institutions and practices of government and in the affairs of daily life. Yet virtually no nation that has undergone a transition from dictatorship to democracy has been entirely successful in resolving these problems.

In working toward these goals, the poverty of structural imagination acts as an inhibiting factor in an age in which the focus of social innovation and ideological controversy around the world has begun to shift away from the old quarrels about statism and privatism and toward an emerging experimentalist rivalry among alternative institutionalized versions of economic and political pluralism. For example, the dominant political regimes of the less-developed economies, and even their critics, often start with the desire merely to imitate and import the institutional arrangements of the rich industrial democracies. These countries take this approach in the hope that from similar institutional devices similar economic and political consequences will result. In practice, however, imitation has not led to the desired results. The failure of these efforts at emulation may, nevertheless, be useful in the development of new institutional structures. Put another way, such efforts may end up driving less-developed political economies into an involuntary institutional experimentalism, which may shed light on the suppressed opportunities for transformation. So it is possible that if Haiti begins on this path, positive results will follow.

Predictions about the success of any political process, and particularly the process of change in Haiti, however, are problematic at best. Therefore, I do not intend to make such predictions. I shall, however, discuss briefly some of the most prominent features of democratic consolidation and apply these features to the circumstances in Haiti. These aspects of the transition process are useful in formulating predictions on which depend the claim that the transition to democracy in Haiti can succeed.

The first significant feature of the consolidation that may occur in Haiti is that the democratization process must take place during one of the worst economic and social crises in the history of the country. In general, this crisis manifests itself in enormously high rates of human rights abuses, including murders, disappearances, and torture, very high unemployment rates, unacceptably high increases in infant mortality, epidemics, and a variety of other social catastrophes. Furthermore, there is great controversy in the international community about whether this crisis may lead to changes in the economic and social structures of Haiti that are necessary to revitalize the economy. The great unknown factor is whether the previous dominant economic groups will remain all powerful or instead have been reduced to mere puppets of the military. During most of Haiti's history the military did the bidding of the elite classes by protecting their economic monopolies and brutally suppressing the vast majority of the poor. In turn, the rich paid off the dictators. But after the 1991 coup the military took over the country's ports and landing strips and as a consequence prospered in the illicit drug trade. Even more significant, the military increasingly prospered through its control of state monopolies, such as the telephone company. For example, Colonel François took over from the rich the old monopolies in flour, sugar, rice, and cement. The military's voraciousness caused some of the traditional economic elite to support the Governors Island Agreement. But the question remains: What will this economic elite do now that Aristide is returned to power?

It is possible that if international aid is forthcoming, Haiti will be able to streamline its economic structure to create more efficient schemes of production and, thus, improve all sectors of society. But, of course, such a possibility requires massive changes in the Haitian economic, political, and social structure. These changes would need to encompass, at a minimum, an overhaul of the tax system to redistribute wealth, strategies to overcome the internal division of Haiti into two or more weakly connected economies, the imposition of real competition on the private sector, and massive investment in people and infrastructure, all backed by the strength of the international community.

A second and integrally connected feature of the consolidation is the required transformation of the corporatist political and social structure that characterizes Haiti. This corporatism has been described as bifrontal. On the one hand, it serves the state by allowing it to control different sectors of civil society; on the other hand, it involves the establishment of cleavages of privilege and domination by different social groups within the structure of the state. The groups that form the constellation of corporative power in Haiti include the armed forces; the Catholic Church; trade groups; a variety of civic organizations, including peasant associations; grass-roots development projects; independent radio stations and the like; and the economic elite. Unlike many nations that have attempted to make the transition from dictatorship to democracy, Haiti's civil society is extremely advanced. Moreover, political parties are among the least advanced parts of this civil society. The strength of civil society is to be found in its diversity and breadth outside electoral politics.

The armed forces and their civilian front (attachés) consolidated their rule by ruthlessly suppressing Haiti's once diverse and vibrant civil society. The military systematically repressed virtually all forms of independent associations in an attempt to deny the Haitian people any organized base for opposition to the dictatorship and to push Haiti back into an atomized and fearful society reminiscent of the Duvalier era. The strategy appeared to be that even if Aristide was returned to power, he would have great difficulty transforming his popularity into the organized support he would need to exert civilian control over the Army and to create a democratic institutional structure that could aid in that endeavor.

Rule of Law and Judicial Independence

Strongly interconnected with the economic, social, political, and institutional aspects is a third feature of the process of democratic consolidation: the deficiency in the fulfillment of the requirements of the rule of law. This deficiency pervades Haiti, acting as an inhibiting incubus to any possible positive democratic development.

Haiti does not, however, lack a comprehensive legal structure that would support a democracy. The blueprint is set forth in the 1987 Constitution, which the Haitian people overwhelmingly approved in a March 29, 1987 election. The Constitution contains specific guarantees of personal liberty and political and civil rights. It provides citizens with the basic freedoms associated with a democratic state: the right to life (article 19), freedom of expression (article 28), freedom of association and assembly (article 31), freedom of the press (article 28-1), and freedom of religion and conscience (article 30). The Constitution also provides citizens protection from prosecution, arrest, or detention unless pursuant to law (article 24-1). For example, no one may be detained without a warrant unless caught in the act of committing a crime, and no arrest may be made between 6 P.M. and 6 A.M. (articles 24-2 and 24-3d). No one may be kept under arrest for more than forty-eight hours without being brought before a judge, who must rule on the legality of the arrest and detention (article 26). Article 276-2 expands all of these protections, providing that all international treaties ratified by Haiti are incorporated directly into Haitian law and supersede any laws in conflict with them. This provision is significant because Haiti has ratified several international human rights conventions.

Despite these provisions, the Haitian judicial system is in disarray. The nation needs not only to develop institutions but to train large numbers of people to run the institutions. Even more ominous for the success of any possible transition to democracy is the fact that Haiti's institutional structure particularly its judicial structure is less developed than that of virtually any nation which has attempted this precarious transition. The majority of judicial officials fail to apply the law because they are intimidated, corrupt, or incompetent. The problem is even more deeply rooted. Deeds of corruption by the highest government officials (the military) occurred daily during the coup years, yet judicial procedures did not prove helpful in investigating these acts.

Perhaps even more destructive to the creation of a democracy than these sources of corruption, however, was the domination by the military dictatorship of all other state power and branches of government. The military monopolized the civilian justice system to such an extent that it failed to investigate or identify the persons responsible for massive human rights violations. There was no judicial independence. Judges were appointed and removed at the will of the military. Per sons arrested or detained by the military had no access to judicial protection. Judges themselves have been detained and beaten for ruling against members of the military. Moreover, attorneys have been harassed, threatened, and even murdered. The armed forces routinely ignored judicial orders, including orders to arrest soldiers or officers accused of human rights violations.

The violation of legal norms, however, is not restricted to the military coup leaders or their supporting cast. Unfortunately, such behavior is a distinguishing mark of Haitian political and social life that has been evident throughout the nation's history. Failure to follow the rule of law is apparent both in social practice and in the actions of government bodies. The tendency to unlawfulness infects not only public officials but the general society, and it correlates with a general trend toward anomie. It manifests itself in such matters as corruption in private economic activities, nonobservance of efficient economic norms, and noncompliance with the most basic rules of society. This general tendency toward illegality in public and social life normally manifests itself in one of two ways: People in Haiti may adopt a "finalist attitude," where they agree with the goals of a rule but do not follow the commands of the rule. Conversely, they may adopt a "formalistic attitude," where they blindly comply with the commands of the rule but ignore the goals. Both attitudes are incompatible with and thus contribute to the continuing difficulty of securing adherence to the rule of law.

The problem is even more complicated. The tendency toward unlawfulness in Haitian public and social life is often the product and the cause of collective action problems, like those that game theory labels "prisoner's dilemma," "assurance game," "chicken game," and so forth. Frequently, the combination of expectations, interests, possibilities of actions, and their respective payoffs are such that the rational course of action for each participant in the process of political or social interaction advises the person not to comply with a certain norm. This is so despite the fact that general compliance with the norm would have been for the benefit of everybody, or almost everybody. Anomie of this kind may be called dumb anomie because it refers to situations in which compliance with a certain norm would have led the social actors to a more efficient result in Pareto's terms than what they obtain in the actual situation of not observing norms.

Moreover, dumb anomie is connected with the stunting of Haiti's economic and social development. First, there is a direct conceptual connection between that kind of anomie and failures in economic productivity. Indeed, dumb anomie is identified by the inefficient results of processes of interaction, including economic ones, that do not observe certain norms. Second, it is clear that anomie affects the process of capital accumulation. For example, when the behavior of people intervening in the process of production-even that of judges and government officials is not sufficiently predictable, productive investments decline or claim disproportionate profits.

Therefore, it is critical for the life of the Haitian nation to consolidate the rule of law. This is important not only to secure respect for fundamental rights and for the observance of the democratic process but also to achieve satisfactory degrees of economic and social development. Moreover, it is obvious that the consolidation of the rule of law, with the consequent overcoming of dumb anomie, requires strengthening the independence, reliability, and efficiency of the judicial process.

The macropolitics of institutional change in Haiti remains inadequate to the aims of democratization and practical experimentalism unless it is complemented by a micropolitics that confronts the logic of habitual social interactions. Haitian culture appears to be strongly resistant to the internalization of universal standards of achievement and competition that are necessary to an equitably functioning democracy. Rather, Haitians appear to have internalized a belief in the overpowering importance of status and connections, thus crippling the transition to a constitutional democracy. In Haitian society there is a predominance of patron-client relations, with their pervasive mingling, in the same associations and encounters, of exchange, power, and sentimental allegiance. There is frequently an oscillation between rule formalism and personal favoritism, and each creates the opportunity and the need for the other. Finally, there is a stark contrast between the treatment of *insiders* (anyone with whom, by virtue of the role you occupy, you have a preexisting relationship) and *outsiders* (everyone else) and the consequent shortage of impersonal respect and reliability.

A "transformative" politics capable of challenging and changing both the established arrangements of the economy and the polity and the intimate habits of sociability must combine a strategic approach to the satisfaction of recognized material interests with the visionary invocation of a reordered society. In Haiti, a nation trapped in these impoverished visions, nothing is more important than to encourage the belief in the Haitian people that structural change is possible.

Coming to Terms with the Past

One way to begin enlarging the collective sense of the possible and to achieve some of the other suggested goals making the rule of law an essential part of public and private life, changing the habits of social interaction, and creating viable democratic institutions is to address the question of how to deal with the massive human rights violations committed by the military dictatorship. These cases involve what Kant referred to as "radical evil" offenses against humanity that are so widespread, persistent, and organized that normal moral assessments seem inadequate.

Hannah Arendt claimed that we know very little about these offenses and that they exhibit a structural element in the realm of human affairs, which is that "men are unable to forgive what they cannot punish and that they are unable to punish what has turned out to be unforgivable." She concluded that these offenses, for which we can neither punish people nor forgive them, "transcend the realm of human affairs and the potentialities of human power, both of which they radically destroy wherever they make their appearance."

This image of powerlessness in the face of these deeds may seem at first sight as merely a literary image that reflects our awe of the inadequacy of human justice and social evolution and its punishments for such deeds. But when actual cases of massive human rights abuses are analyzed, it becomes clear that there are strong barriers to going forward even with measures that are applied to common criminals.

One problem, on a level of moral assessment, is the possibility that the persons who commit these acts have concepts, such as "the natural good," which are incomprehensible to us and lead to actions that are incommensurable under our conceptual schemes. This poses the problem of whether a state can legitimately carry out moral discourse outside its boundaries and thus subject agents who do not share the assumptions of that discourse to courses of action based on its findings. This problem, of course, destroys any possibility of grounding public moral responsibility in consensus because even moral disagreement is foreclosed by conceptual divergence.

Other moral problems exist even if the problem of conceptual relativism is overcome. For example, the type of collective behavior that is necessary for the commission of these acts would not have been successful without strong conviction by the perpetrators of the deeds. Sincere conviction poses problems for moral evaluations even if the society does not agree with the substantive content of the conviction. Moreover, the mistaken character of the conviction has to be demonstrated. This, of course, raises questions about the foundations of human rights and about their scope and balance when several of them conflict.

Another moral problem concerns the diffusion of responsibility. These deeds cannot be committed without the assent of numerous and very different people in the society. There are those who planned the acts and those who executed them. There are those who in some way supported the actions by giving information to the perpetrators or by lending material support. Indeed, this assent even includes the eventual victims. There are also a large number of people who cooperated by acts of omission: Are we to punish all of the numerous judges who failed to enforce the rule of law; journalists who failed to report on the atrocities; diplomats who concealed or attempted to justify the position of their governments; and everyday citizens who decided to turn a blind eye to what was happening, refrained from telling other people about the atrocities, or even justified the deeds? To reach this point leads to the view that if almost everyone had some complicity in these acts, then everyone is guilty and thus nobody is guilty.

This set of moral concerns translates into political and legal considerations that the Aristide government must face in any attempt to take action against the military. The conditions under which Aristide has resumed office will, of course, determine in part the limits of the possible. Whether or not the shape of the amnesty agreed upon at Governors Island remains intact under new conditions is a key unknown factor as of this writing as is the extent to which other measures of purge, investigation, or reparations will be possible. Clearly, there will be no prosecutions for the coup itself or for affronts against democracy. But what about the crimes that under international law cannot be subject to a blanket amnesty? The direct incorporation of international human rights treaties into Haitian law gives rise to an obligation on the government's part to take action against the individuals who have assassinated, caused to disappear, tortured, and arbitrarily jailed thousands of Haitians. Complying with that obligation will require staunch international and domestic support. But even assuming the best possible scenario, significant impediments remain to prosecutions or even to investigations of the abuses that were committed.

A key problem is defining the chain of responsibility for both criminal and civil purposes. Although the military has a clear-cut command structure, the relationship among the military, the police, and the "attachés" and other private goon squads is less clear for purposes of attributing both state and command responsibility. The lines of communication between the coup leaders and the attachés and rural section heads are ambiguous the attachés and section chiefs are adjuncts who both receive orders and act independently. Nonetheless, a plausible argument can be made that these individuals have over time become agents of the state, so that all their actions may be attributed to the state. A similar problem arises with respect to members of the economic elite who bankrolled and otherwise supported the coup and who may have been involved in death squad-type activities. Should these individuals be held criminally or civilly liable for the results of their actions?

In October 1993, with the Governors Island accord still in place and Aristide's return to Haiti imminent, the democratic government convened a group of international experts to help it, as a priority, elucidate a policy on human rights trials, among other issues. With the assassination of Minister of Justice Malary and the disintegration of the accord, the seminar never took place. Presently, with a new limited amnesty law in place, President Aristide continues to stress the need for national reconciliation as well as for justice. He has established a National Commission for Truth and Justice, whose mandate will be to establish worldwide the truth with regards to all serious violations of human rights committed between September 29, 1991 and October 5, 1994, both in the interior as well as abroad against all

Haitians, provided that these violations are related with the Haitian state or Haitian politics.

Still, both the promise and the paradoxes of coming to terms with the past remain unexplored.

The transformation of Haitian society is fraught with many dangers. How the Haitians deal with these massive human rights crimes of the past will not pose the least of these dangers. The answers to these issues will indeed help determine whether and to what extent Haiti will become a viable democracy.

Bibliography

Aaronson, Susan Ariel and Jamie M. Zimmerman. *Trade Imbalance: The Struggle to Weigh Human Rights Concerns in Trade Policymaking.* Cambridge, UK: Cambridge University Press, 2007.

Agosín, Marjorie, ed. *Women, Gender, and Human Rights: A Global Perspective.* New Brunswick, NJ: Rutgers University Press, 2001

Baderin, Mashood A. *International Human Rights and Islamic Law.* New York: Oxford University Press, 2003.

Bae, Sangmin. *When the State No Longer Kills: International Human Rights Norms and Abolition of Capital Punishment.* Albany, NY: State University Press of New York, 2007.

Campbell, Tom, Jeffrey Goldsworthy, and Adrienne Stone, eds. *Protecting Human Rights: Instruments and Institutions.* New York: Oxford University Press, 2003.

Caney, Simon and Peter Jones, ed. *Human Rights and Global Diversity.* London: Frank Cass, 2001.

Cardenas, Sonia. *Conflict and Compliance: State Responses to International Human Rights Pressure.* Philadelphia, PA: University of Pennsylvania Press, 2007

de Wet, Erika. *The Constitutional Enforceability of Economic and Social Rights: The Meaning of the German Constitutional Model for South Africa.* London: Butterworth- Heinemann, 1996.

Dijk, Pieter van. *Theory and Practice of the European Convention on Human Rights.* The Hague: Kluwer Law International, 1998.

Donnelly, Jack. *Human Rights in Theory & Practice.* Ithaca, NY: Cornell University Press, 2nd ed., Cornell University Press, 2003.

Eldridge, Phil. *Politics of Human Rights in Southeast Asia.* London: Routledge, 2002.

Emberland, Marius. *The Human Rights of Companies: Exploring the Structure of ECHR Protection.* New York: Oxford University Press, 2006.

Falk, Richard A. *Human Rights Horizons: The Pursuit of Justice in a Globalizing World.* New York: Routledge, 2000.

Flekkøy, Målfrid Grude and Natalie Hevener Kaufman. *The Participation Rights of the Child: Rights and Responsibilities in Family and Society.* London: Jessica Kingsley Publ., 1997.

Gearty, Conor. *Principles of Human Rights Adjudication.* New York: Oxford University Press, 2004.

Gearty, Conor. *Can Human Rights Survive?* Cambridge, UK: Cambridge University Press, 2006.

Harris, David and Stephen Livingstone, eds. *The Inter-American System of Human Rights.* New York: Oxford University Press, 1998.

Harrison, James. *The Human Rights Impact of the World Trade Organisation.* Oxford, UK: Hart, 2007.

Ife, Jim. *Human Rights and Social Work: Towards Rights-Based Practice.* Cambridge, UK: Cambridge University Press, 2001.

James, Stephen. *Universal Human Rights: Origins and Development.* New York: LFB Scholarly Publ., 2007.

Janis, Mark, Richard Kay, and Anthony Bradley. *European Human Rights Law: Texts and Materials.* New York: Oxford University Press, 2nd ed., 2001.

Keal, Paul. *European Conquest and the Rights of Indigenous Peoples: The Moral Backwardness of International Society.* Cambridge, UK: Cambridge University Press, 2003.

Kent, Ann E. *China, the United Nations, and Human Rights: The Limits of Compliance.* Philadelphia, PA: University of Pennsylvania Press, 1999.

Landman, Todd. *Protecting Human Rights: A Comparative Study.* Washington, DC: Georgetown University Press, 2005.

Madigan, Janet Holl. *Truth, Politics, and Universal Human Rights.* New York: Palgrave Macmillan, 2007.

Neyroud, Peter and Alan Beckley. *Policing, Ethics and Human Rights.* Portland, OR: Willan Publ., 2001.

Oestreich, Joel E. *Power and Principle: Human Rights Programming in International Organizations.* Washington, DC: Georgetown University Press, 2007.

Pasqualucci, Jo M. *The Practice and Procedure of the Inter-American Court of Human Rights.*Cambridge, UK: Cambridge University Press, 2003.

Ramcharan, B.G. *The Security Council and the Protection of Human Rights.* The Hague: Kluwer Law International, 2002.

Salman, Salman M.A. and Siobahn McInerney-Lankford. *The Human Right to Water: Legal and Policy Dimensions.* Washington, DC: The International Bank for Reconstruction and Development/The World Bank, 2004.

Talbott, William J. *Which Rights Should Be Universal?* New York: Oxford University Press, 2005.

Umozurike, Oji. *The African Charter on Human and Peoples' Rights.* The Hague: Nijhoff, 1997.

Weisburd, A. Mark. *Comparative Human Rights Law, Vol. 1: Expression, Association, Religion.* Durham, NC: Carolina Academic Press, 2007.

Index

V

W

Z